# The Untold Story Of Western Civilization

# Vol. 1

# The Untold Story Of Western Civilization

Volume I:

## Prehistory/The Matriarchy

The Age of the Mothers

Chuck & Tom Paprocki

InnerWorld Publications
San Germán, Puerto Rico
www.innerworldpublications.com

Copyright 2018 by Charles Paprocki & Tom Paprocki

All rights reserved under International and Pan-American Copyright Conventions

Published in the United States by InnerWorld Publications
P.O. Box 1613, San Germán, Puerto Rico, 00683

Library of Congress Control Number: 2018948333

ISBN: 9781881717676

Cover Design:

All rights reserved. This book, or parts thereof, may not be reproduced in any form or by any means, electronic or mechanical, including photocopying, recording, or by any information storage or retrieval system, without permission of the publisher except for brief quotations.

# DEDICATION

To the memory of Prabhat Rainjan Sarkar,
our spiritual guide and revolutionary mentor

# Contents

INTRODUCTION . . . . . . . . . . . . . . . . . . . . . . . . . . . . . . . 1

    The Thirst for Limitlessness . . . . . . . . . . . . . . . . . . 11
    Social Psychology . . . . . . . . . . . . . . . . . . . . . . . . . . 15
    Men and Women . . . . . . . . . . . . . . . . . . . . . . . . . . 16

Matriarchy, the Goddess
and Her Consort . . . . . . . . . . . . . . . . . . . . . . . . . . . . . 21

    The Time of the Matriarchy . . . . . . . . . . . . . . . . . . 22
    The Clan . . . . . . . . . . . . . . . . . . . . . . . . . . . . . . . . 26
    The Moon and the Mystery of Motherhood . . . . . . 28
    The Great Goddess . . . . . . . . . . . . . . . . . . . . . . . . 31
    The Virgin and the Serpent . . . . . . . . . . . . . . . . . . 34
    Blood Sacrifice . . . . . . . . . . . . . . . . . . . . . . . . . . . 37
    The Sacred King . . . . . . . . . . . . . . . . . . . . . . . . . . 38
    Brother Rule . . . . . . . . . . . . . . . . . . . . . . . . . . . . 50
    The Husband . . . . . . . . . . . . . . . . . . . . . . . . . . . . 56
    Fatherhood . . . . . . . . . . . . . . . . . . . . . . . . . . . . . 62
    Partitioning the Firstborn . . . . . . . . . . . . . . . . . . . 66

The Rise of Patriarchy . . . . . . . . . . . . . . . . . . . . . . . . 70

    The Bride Price . . . . . . . . . . . . . . . . . . . . . . . . . . 71
    The Father-Family . . . . . . . . . . . . . . . . . . . . . . . . 76
    Classification of Married Women . . . . . . . . . . . . . 78

Aryans – the First Patriarchs . . . . . . . . . . . . . . . . . . 81

    The Start of Patriarchal Religion . . . . . . . . . . . . . . 82

| | |
|---|---:|
| The Invasion of the Indus Valley by the Aryans | 91 |
| Slavery and Racism | 99 |
| The Aryan Caste System | 103 |

## Lord Shiva and the Birth of Mysticism — 107

| | |
|---|---:|
| Shiva's Legacy | 110 |
| The Meaning of "Shiva" | 112 |
| The Gifts of Shiva | 114 |
|    A Marriage of Mutual Respect | 114 |
|    The Octave, Mudra, and Dance | 115 |
|    Medical Science | 116 |
|    Care for Plants and Animals | 116 |
|    Spiritual Science: Tantric Yoga | 118 |

## Notes — 122

## Index — 129

# INTRODUCTION

*The farther backward you can look, the farther forward you are likely to see.*
— Winston S. Churchill

People say a lot of things about history and what its value is. The purpose of our particular history is to uncover the roots of our programming, to see why we think and believe the way we do today and how our "feelings" about other people came to be. While this book covers the flow of Western civilization, the same patterns exist in Eastern and Southern civilizations. This is because we are all human beings, provided with the same tools and response mechanisms by which to decipher and control our existence.

How do we know ourselves? On what basis do we judge our neighbors? Normally, when we want to identify someone, we seek to answer certain basic questions about them. What is their gender, race, class, nationality, and religion. While there are others factors; for instance, our age, job, or political persuasion, these are the fundamental descriptors by which we identify each other as human beings. Each one of these descriptors is charged with a profound meaning which has resulted from the largely subconscious thoughts, emotions, and sentiments that lie behind them. In our interactions with people, we relate to them through this subconscious programming instead of to them directly. This means that we cannot see each other as human beings because we have covered each other over with preconceptions based upon our programming. For the well-wishers of human society who want to improve the human condition, we need to bring our subconscious social programming into consciousness.

For example, let's say that as a man living in the United States at the beginning of the twenty-first century, I come to believe that women are superior to men and not vice-versa. This would challenge most men's programming that they are superior to women. As a man, such a violation of my subconscious programming might even diminish my sense of self when I look into a mirror in the morning. If I looked into the eyes of another man, I might see something different from what I had seen my whole life. By saying that "women are superior to men," I rock the boat. My subconscious programming is painfully disrupted. To avoid this pain and confusion, it is much easier to maintain my subconscious sentiments about men and women than to challenge them. When I disturb my complacency, I become fearful of the fact that I must now examine so many accepted other thoughts and beliefs that I had in the past.

I also become a threat to others. Those who know me become fearful. They feel the need to reassert their belief about men and women without ever considering the reasons behind their beliefs. They get angry because my questioning challenges their unquestioned beliefs. It is only natural that people require stability in their environment; nonetheless, if we want to escape our mental prison and be more human than we presently are, we must confront our social conditioning.

Rationally, there are many ways in which women are superior to men and this fact does not make me any less as a human being. Rather in admitting such, it makes me more of a human being and helps me create a more balanced view of reality. It actually allows me to make spiritual progress.

Take the question of nationality. If I believe that the United States is the best nation on earth because of my programming, I am less apt to look at the whole picture when the United States invades another nation. I am more susceptible to believe what the mass media tells me, instead of seeking the truth.

Therefore, if the religious and political dogmas that control our programming are not brought to consciousness and exposed for what they are, we will not be able to address our situation in a rational manner. We will not be able to interact with people in the manner that is required, nor manifest the future we desire. Rather, we will unconsciously continue to make the same mistakes as we have in the past and get angry over the fact that people do not think the way we want them to think. We are all caught in the matrix of our social programming. And this matrix is a result of our collective history.

As human beings we share certain characteristics with plants and animals. Much of our DNA is no different from that of a plant. Of course, with the more evolved species, like primates, we share not only biological attributes, but also mental characteristics. We have instincts, emotions and sentiments in common. We possess the desire for food, shelter, rest, sex, love, etc. Scientists have long established the fact that our brain is composed of the limbic system and the mammalian brain, which indicates our connection to all land-based species in the evolutionary process. As humans, though, we also possess unique qualities and a unique addition to our brain, the cerebral cortex. This allow us to think rationally, a talent not available to other species. As human beings, it is incumbent upon us to develop our higher qualities, not only for ourselves but also because the human race depends upon us. We are in an ideological flow with all of humanity whether we realize it or not.

We are all moving within the natural flow of the evolutionary process. In this process, it is our nature to want to be more. To do so, we must have our basic needs met and have the opportunity to think freely. In this way, we expand our minds. In order to *be* more, and not just *do* more or *have* more, we need to serve our fellow beings in a selfless manner. This gives us the experience of love, the most powerful yet delicate and rare quality of life. It is only by coming to understand and experience love, that we are able to fulfill our ultimate destiny of attaining eternal happiness.

No human being wants to become degraded or to be treated as less than they are. To develop and prosper in life is a natural desire for human beings. Yet, our history reveals that some fulfill this desire by degrading others. They prosper at the expense of others. They do not care if they move far ahead leaving others in the dust and misery. Our heroes, however, are those people who have moved together with the rest of society, sharing our knowledge and our strength. They understand in their hearts that as human beings we must look out for each other. There is no glory in becoming great at the expense of others. Nonetheless, most histories have been written to glorify those who have done just that—the warlords, the bishops, and the CEOs who have become fat by impoverishing others.

It is not the intention of this history book to glorify such people. We really do not care who succeeded whom on the throne, or who became a bishop to extort the wealth of others, or what capitalist plundered the people's labor and resources. Such parasites do not inspire others to greatness. In the writing of our history, therefore, we have not looked to glorify such people, but to understand the consequences of their actions on our collective subconscious. We have also sought to find those who have made contributions to the advancement of humanity as a whole. People who inspire us and give us hope. Those, who struggle to help others and who hold out hope in times of desperation, are the people we want to know about.

Therefore, as we uncover the historical roots of our social programming, we must decide whether this programming derived from those who sought our best interests or from those who had their own selfish agenda. In this way, we will be able to judge who contributed to our progress and who took advantage of us for personal gain. If only a handful of people out of billions reach the pinnacle of wealth and power, this has never benefited the human race as a whole. Rather, given the fact that resources are finite, those few who commandeer the majority of the wealth for themselves only impoverish the people as a whole. Thereby, they keep us from developing according to our inner human nature.

As we researched the story of Western Civilization, we were continually confronted with the question of whether we could trust what we read or was it a false narrative created by the ruling classes of the day to mislead and misinform. We soon realized that we can only come to a semblance of truth through study and using our rational minds. In trying to do this, we used original source materials whenever possible and also read a variety of opinions concerning each historical period in order to determine if these sources were in consort with other known facts or whether they were presented as truth to make some king or priest look good. We have also tried to balance the viewpoints of a white male dominated history with that of what others were doing within the examined periods of time.

Originally, we intended to begin our search for the roots of our current Pax Americana programming with the Protestant Reformation that gave rise to the dominant religious and political beliefs of today's European countries and the United States. We would then have proceeded to the Enlightenment period beginning around 1800 where, after a century of religious wars that ravaged Europe, it finally became apparent that the role of religion in social decision-making had to be curtailed for the betterment of society as a whole. During the Enlightenment period, freedom of thought prevailed after centuries of religious dogma and superstition and because of this, the western world experienced a rebirth of philosophy, science, the arts, and political thought. By beginning our story with the Reformation and the Enlightenment, we would be able to understand our contemporary political viewpoints and our religious viewpoints as well. We would be able to observe the birth of capitalism and see how the political values of liberty, democracy, representative government, the separation of church and state, etc., were formed. We would witness the birth of the European nation states and the legal codes that gave rise to representative government. We would observe the rise of the bourgeoisie, the urban merchants, and see how those who possessed the merchant psychology became the ruling class of society. We would also see how the apparatus for monetizing every object and every action set in motion the current juggernaut that completely ignores the existence of eco-systems and planetary life support systems that are responsible for human existence. We would see how our programming makes it acceptable for corporations to continue to destroy the earth in the name of profit. We would see how our exaggerated national patriotism took root.

By looking back to the Reformation and the Enlightenment period, we would also see the birth of current social philosophies, the left-wing liberalism and right wing conservatism that motivate the current political system. We would be able to see how these ideas proved vital in the past, but, under current conditions, are unable to resolve the individual, social, and environmental problems that are now leading us to destruction.

Knowing the roots of our religious, political, and economic systems is vital to our understanding of our current condition. Knowing their weaknesses and limitations is required to understand why we need a new ideology if we truly value the common needs of humanity and the entire planet. Our military technology and our economic juggernaut are destroying civilization and the very life-support systems of the planet; yet we do not know how *not* to do this. We are governed by ideas and institutions that are leading to our own destruction, and we have no holistic worldview, no universal ideology, to guide our movement out of this mess.

In our deliberations of how to write this history, we came to realize that it is not enough just to have a religious or political-economic analysis of our condition. This limited point of view is part of the trap that keeps us focused on church and nation-state and unable to search for answers outside of them. Human beings are much more than our beliefs in these institutions. Such institutions are only a few hundred years old, and yet as human beings we have been on a march together for over a million years. Deep within our collective psychology are beliefs that were formed millennia ago that continue to affect our vision of life and affect our progress as a species. These beliefs, in fact, go back to the pre-historic period, to a time before patriarchy when the mothers and their brothers formed the values, politics, and economics of the clan, and later the clan confederation, tribes, and nations. This happened millennia before city-states, church states, or nation states and well before private property and the father family that constitute the beginnings of patriarchal society. If we want to understand the source of our current predicament regarding sex and gender, we will have to first understand our human nature is expressed by both men and women. To do this, we shall have to go back to the period of the matriarchy, to a time when women, in their role of mothers, created the Great Goddess, magic, blood sacrifice, the sacred king, mathematics, astrology, etc., that lead to the making of the great agricultural civilizations of the Indus Valley, Mesopotamia, and Egypt.

Without such an undertaking, we will never be able to see what a society looks like when women play the dominant role. We will remain unable to free our minds from our destructive programming regarding gender relations. We will remain unable to share a vision of a better world and work together as men and women to create it. Just as children must know their parents to be healthy individuals, so humanity must know our ancestors to be a healthy society. Our vision of a better world will not be served by creating some patriarchal religious or politically utopian vision of life devoid of a deep appreciation of gender equality. Such a utopian vision would only lead to failure and we do not have the time to fail. We cannot afford to waste people's time. The essential *who, what, when, where,* and *why* of our future depends upon what we understand about ourselves in the present moment and this cannot be determined unless we understand what we have been through together.

Having said this, we anticipate that many historians will attack us for our thoroughly *unhistorical* approach. We apologize to the scholars, but we are more interested in our past than we are of our history as an academic discipline. Our history is not written for the student of history. It is written for the social activist within each of us. It is a call to stir our inner greatness.

We also know that our history is only a story like all other histories. While based on "facts," we know that facts in history are scarce, and like pieces of a puzzle, they need to be assembled to tell a story. This is difficult because each fact, whether it is written in script or exists in archeological artifacts, is currently debated from every possible angle with every interpretation serving the interpreter's agenda; as well as it should. As such, there is not just one interpretation of history, but many. Of course, as we move closer to the present there tends to be greater scientific consensus, but in the ancient past, when politics and mythology mixed with religion to interpret events, the meaning of facts can quickly transform. With each historian that graduates from college, another history is created. Even given the same historical "facts," vast differences in interpretation exist. Chronologies differ widely; places that no longer exist are attributed to different locations on the map. The lives of people are distorted for a myriad of reasons either by their peers or later writers for political reasons that we no longer are able to grasp. Even great personalities get lost when we go seeking for facts. Did Moses exist? Historians say unlikely. Did Jesus Christ exist? If he did, he is not the person we have come to worship in the American twenty-first century.

We say these things with caution. We admire historians greatly and know that we must seek constantly to know our past because without knowing the past, we cannot understand the present. We cannot decipher truth from fiction, or, more significantly, we cannot tell truth from the dogmas that have shackled our minds for centuries and continue to keep us from evolving as human beings.

The story that follows is intended to present a flow of history from approximately thirty-five thousand years ago until the present. In presenting this flow, we have assembled widely accepted facts from across time and place and have arranged them in a particular pattern to give us a big picture of our evolution as human beings. Specifically, we look at how people thought about God, nature, and each other and how their interpretations gave rise to our current social conditions.

For the sake of brevity, we have concentrated on the evolution of the western world and the creation of Western Civilization. This should in no way be considered a slight to people of other civilizations or races, for in their stories of human history, we find, as a general rule, a more humane and spiritually-orientation lifestyle. In the Far East, the people knew about the "One God" millennia before it was discovered in the West. From the time of Shiva, it grew into the social consciousness of the people of India, was refreshed by Lord Krishna and Lord Buddha, taken to China by Bodhidharma, and then transferred by monks to Japan and other countries of the Far East. After centuries of yogic practices, the cultures of the Far East have been suffused with spiritual consciousness.

In Africa, before the coming of the white colonialists and slave traders, the people lived a life similar to the people in the Middle East. Africa was an exotic garden in which great empires, royal courts, stone palaces, intricate art, and gold jewelry were created. Empires emerged, declined, and intermixed. When Europe was going through its Dark Ages, the empires of Africa were going through a continental Renaissance. The leading civilizations of this African rebirth were the Axum Empire, the Kingdom of Ghana, the Mali Empire, the Songhai Empire, the Ethiopian Empire, the Mossi Kingdoms and the Benin Empire.[1] Historians and archeologists have been remiss in putting together this grand story, focusing instead only on Egypt and Nubia, which were largely part of the history of the Middle East and thus participants in the development of Western Civilization.

We can never forget that the birth of humanity occurred in Africa. The African people are our most ancient ancestors and are worthy of our greatest respect. We would still be dragging our knuckles on the ground if it were not for our African ancestors. We have much to learn from the African people about what it means to be a human being.[2]

The people of the Americas also have a unique history that stretched from about 30,000 BC when their ancestors crossed the Bering Strait, to about AD 1492 with the coming of Christopher Columbus and the slavers. It was around twelve thousand years ago that the glaciers receded in the northern climes and allowed the population to grow and spread throughout the Americas. Many tribes, nations, and civilizations were formed due to the welcoming climate.[3]

Like other people across the planet, they too created great civilizations, built pyramid-temples, invented mathematics, astronomy, medicine, writing, highly accurate calendars, fine arts, intensive agriculture, engineering, an abacus calculator, and complex theologies and social structures. In addition, they used copper, silver, and gold for metalworking. They also created spiritual masters as is evident from the writings of the Sioux, the Yaqui, and the Hopi.

We have also been led to take a closer look at expressions of mysticism or spirituality throughout western history. In doing so, we discovered that it is often within the buried accounts of our history that many secrets lie as to the shape of our current social programming. In revealing these sources, we have been able to see the many sentiments and dogmas that have given shape to what we now complacently accept as "real life."

In the study of our past, we looked at three fundamental characteristics of human consciousness, which, in their unfolding, have largely defined us as human beings. These are: (1) our ingrained thirst for limitlessness, (2) the psychologies we employ to gain power over social and environmental conditions, and (3) the evolution of the mentalities of men and women. These three mental characteristics of human consciousness are largely responsible for initiating our quest for an absolute power. In other words, these psychic urges evolved our ideas of God over time. While it is true that God creates humanity, it is also true that humanity has continually sought to create a better idea of God. In this vein, we will look at the mystical teachings of Lord Shiva (Hinduism), Moses (Judaism), Jesus Christ (Christianity), and the Prophet Mohammed (Islam) while also noting that the religious dogmas that grew up in their wakes were often far removed from original spiritual teaching.

Within social psychology, we will look at the development of the warrior psychology and the phenomenon of empire building, which instituted slavery and gave rise to our current ideas about race. We will look at the intellectual psychology that manifested in the priest class in the Middle Ages and how physical control gave way to psychic control. We will also look at the birth of capitalism and how it created the descriptors of occupation, class, nationality, and political leaning that governs much of our thinking and social behavior today.

## The Thirst for Limitlessness

Human beings are mind-preponderant beings. Our history is more ideological than biological. While other species are mostly governed by their biology, we are governed by our mental propensities—our instincts, sentiments, rationality, and intuition. As such, human history is primarily about how we interpret reality and how we respond to it. In the simplest terms, human history reflects our desire to move from imperfection to perfection—to be more. We move from animality toward Divinity. This evolutionary process is driven by our thirst for limitlessness.

For most people, the ultimate state of perfection (unlimited happiness or love) is embodied in our definition of God. This definition of God evolved over time. It began simply in hearing the voices of the creatures around us and the voices of our ancestors in our heads. It then evolved into fertility goddesses and then gods that represented the forces of nature. In time, after we developed a subjective consciousness, our gods and goddesses became totally anthropomorphic, sharing all of our passions and foibles, but nonetheless always having more power than humans. With Zoroastrianism the theory of two gods emerged, one good and one bad, simplifying the vast pantheons that were worshipped by previous civilizations. Finally, with the Jews, the idea of one God, monotheism, emerged. Yet monotheism as a philosophical concept is not the last step in the process of understanding the Divine. If it were, there would not be different definitions of the One God in whose cause we kill heretics, and wage religious wars. There would not be any "my One God is greater than your One God." Thus, we can say that the One God who is worshiped by the majority of people is not the One God, but only the one god of one's particular religion.

Logically, if there is a One God, nothing that *is* or *is not* would exist outside it. If something existed outside the One God, it would no longer be the One God, because it would not contain everything within itself. For the One God there is no inside nor outside, no *is* or *is not*. All the dualities that the mind conceives are resolved in the Oneness of God Consciousness.

Most people do not comprehend God as universal consciousness because they think that while there is the One God, the universe exists outside him/her/it. This flaw in human thinking has kept us from advancing as a species for thousands of years. It has allowed religions to control our minds and turn us against each other. Only the mystics understand the One God. Mystics may be of any religion or no religion. They may live in civilization or outside civilization. None of these things matter. The mystic understands that everything in this world is a reflection of a universal consciousness. Just as a ray of sunlight is a reflection of the Sun, so every physical and mental expression in this universe is a reflection of the One God. God is the Universal Consciousness of which everything is a form. And whether we want to call it God,

Universal Consciousness, or any other name, it is our basic human impulse to transcend human limitations and seek the limitless joy that mystics call God-realization.

The difficulty in understanding the One God (Universal Consciousness) is that we think that we can understand it by thinking. Unfortunately, we cannot, because the mind is a limited consciousness that can only operate within the dimension of duality. Whatever thought a mind thinks, its opposite also exists. If I define the One God and you do not agree with my definition, then we have two One Gods and a fight on our hands. Universal Consciousness cannot be defined. To *define* means to identify something as distinct from its environment. By defining something, one intentionally excludes what lies outside of the definition.

This is why religions will never lead us to understand Universal Consciousness, why they continually foment distinctions between their followers and others. This is why religious leaders continually fall prey to the desire for wealth and power, as do all other organizations. This is why current religious ideologies are two small to inspire humanity as a whole.

The masses of people are drawn to spiritual masters because of the master's love for them. Spiritual masters, as mystics, hold up the torch that lets us glimpse, within the darkness, a path to perfection. They assure us that our longing for limitlessness is genuine and achievable. It is this same urge, regardless how primitive in expression, that is manipulated by priests and their religions in the name of God. Priest classes are not so much concerned about the self-realization of their faithful as they are about their subservience. Thus, we say that the priests, by and large, reflect the normal way that intellectuals have power. They manipulate our infinite longing with sentimental myths, dogmas, and rituals, and by such means control our minds.

As human beings refined their definition of God and spiritual teachers came along to guide our understanding, mysticism evolved. How is it that the mystics were able to know God? The great mystics of all time have told us that to know God is to love God. The answer is love but how does it work? The mystics sacrificed their lives for the God they love. As is common in every relationship, if you love someone, you will go out of your way to help them. You will not expect anything back. You give of yourself, your time, and your resources in a selfless manner. That person will see the sacrifices that you make and will reciprocate, falling deeper in love with you, inspired to do so because of the greater sacrifices that you have made. It works the same way between the individual and the Universal Consciousness. The mystics understood that if you love God by telling God how much you love Him/Her/It and by demonstrating it by taking care of His/Her/It's creation in a selfless manner, God will love you back. As Jesus said, "Thou shalt love the Lord thy God with all thy heart, and with all thy soul, and with all thy mind." This is the first and greatest commandment. And the second is similiar, "Thou shalt love thy neighbor as thyself." On these two commandments hang all the laws and the prophets. (Matt 22:37-40)

In our history, we will see how this mystery of love gets expressed in the lives of the mystics and how the rich and powerful, be they rulers of states, religions, or corporations always fail to grasp its true importance. Caught up in duality, they become slaves to that which they desire to possess—unlimited wealth and power. Love eludes them and the deepest longing of their being remains unfulfilled. And so their life passes without making any progress in their humanity.

Not knowing how to *be more* through love, human beings remain immature in their approach to Universal Consciousness. We do not understand that the desire to be more is rooted in our deepest level of consciousness and expressed through our heart (intuition). Instead, we think this quest for limitlessness is a product of our minds and bodies. Consequently, we misinterpret it as a drive to "do more" or "have more." This is the fatal flaw that has led us to our present condition. Take a look around you. There are now over seven billion people on this small planet, all wanting to do more and have more. We never stop to consider that our drive to satiate an infinite longing with finite resources is a fool's game that can never be won. It has only led us to global imperialism and the impoverishment of the planetary systems. We will need to come to grips with this mental aberration if we are to salvage our humanity and our planet and build a better future for our children.

## Social Psychology

Reality is physical, mental, and spiritual in nature. Yet, for all practical purposes, we only consider reality to be psycho-physical. As such, we focus on how to control this psycho-physical reality. This is understandable. We cannot survive without having some control over our environment. Thus, the evolution of social psychologies. When we examine the dynamics of power within a historical context, we discover that there are only three ways to have power in this world—control by physical force as the warriors do, control by psychic force as the intellectuals do, or control by money as the merchants do. These three psychologies are reflected in every human culture and in each culture one of these psychologies is always dominant in the ruling class. In their dominance, the ruling class creates the institutions that keep them in power. In ancient history, armies ruled the earth. In the middle ages, the Church ruled. And in modern history, the corporations rule.

The warrior psychology evolved during the periods of prehistory and ancient history because of the struggle to survive physically. This entailed fighting the forces of nature and attacks by other men. Before the creation of clan confederations, there were always other clans in striking distance who could come to steal and kill. As geographic territories grew larger and dangers increased, clan confederations grew into tribes and then into tribal confederations or nations. In time, empires developed to conquer weaker opponents. In the West, our involvement in empire building gave rise to our current programming regarding slavery, race, class, and our national and religious identities.

In the middle ages, the intellectual psychology dominated. This is the time when religion took control of human beings, commanding not only our bodies but also our minds as well. While the Persians, Egyptians, and ancient Turks had their priest class, it was the Jewish priests who set the stage for religious domination in the Western world and who were then followed by the priest classes of the Christians and then the Muslims. As the idea of God became more sophisticated, priests were able to create religious institutions having greater longevity and social control.

In modern and contemporary history, the merchant psychology dominates and everyone is under control of the richest capitalists. Every atom in the universe is given its dollar value and it is virtually impossible to survive without money. When an intellectual devotes all of his time and energy to the acquisition of material wealth, he becomes a capitalist.

## Men and Women

The third theme in our history of Western Civilization is the different ways in which men and women think and act, and how this gives rise to different mentalities and different skills. We will look at what this means when each gender is in a position of decision-making.

Gender relations are the most nuclear relations among human beings. For purposes of self-identification, a person will always acknowledge their gender before any other descriptor. Who am I? I am a woman. This is what women do. Who am I? I am a man. This is what men do. Today men do not perceive women as equals because we do not understand human history. Having been told that we were always superior, we have come to believe it. It is much easier to be full of ourselves and assume that we alone have been responsible for anything worthwhile in history. Women are our property, our sidekicks, the weaker sex. This faulty thinking has led us to the brink of disaster that we now face as a species. We are tragically imbalanced in the way we think and feel as a species. This imbalance is a result of our programming during the age of patriarchy.

An exploration of our past reveals that it was the women who brought us out of animality, defined our humanity, and led us to create the great agricultural civilizations of the world, including Egypt, Mesopotamia, and the Indus Valley. Because most male historians off-handedly dismiss anything before the advent of language and archeological artifacts as "prehistory," not worthy of investigation, they have not been able to understand what went on for the first million years of human existence, prior to the arrival of patriarchy, a mere ten thousand years ago. Granted that there was no script back then, and only a smattering of archeological artifacts (which are the basic tools of historians), it was not easy, nor apparently worthwhile, to understand just how we managed to develop out of the primal horde of mammalian existence, to the full-blown civilizations of the ancient world, prior to the descent of the Nordic Aryan patriarchal tribes onto the lands of India, the Middle East and northern Europe. Thankfully, women historians have begun to put the puzzle together and in doing so have presented humanity with a priceless gift by which we can more fully understand human nature and the path toward our ultimate goal. As a human species, we do have an ultimate goal, and no matter what we call it, in the end, it all refers to the same human impulse to transcend human limitations and achieve unlimited happiness.

Having come through the epochs of ancient, medieval, modern and contemporary history, we are now approaching the end game of patriarchy.

Our human civilization is now global in scope and our impact on the eco-systems and life support systems are planetary in scope. The problems are bigger than we are able to think about, given our lack of foresight. As such, we are quickly approaching a civilizational dead end that will destroy countless lives unless we are willing and able to make a leap forward as human beings. It is not the first time that we have had to make great leaps to survive and it will not be the last. But insofar as our species is concerned, it will be the greatest challenge we have ever faced. And the more that we are prepared, the greater our chance of survival. Our preparation begins with gleaning the knowledge of our past, because in this understanding, we will be able to see the course of our trajectory. Only by understanding our past will we understand our present and be able to shape our future.

To summarize, the purpose of our story is to understand the roots of our subconscious programming regarding gender, race, class, religion, and nationality. These are the qualities by which we identify ourselves. They are the constructs by which we live our lives. And yet, our sentimental attachments to these constructs do not allow us to think for the welfare of the species. We cannot fathom how to think or act for the benefit of the whole of humanity even though our crisis is now global in scope. Because the survival of the entire human race and the life support systems of the planet are at stake, it now becomes vital to understand our fundamental humanity independent of such descriptors. Regardless of our gender, race, class, nation or religious divisions, we need to know what we share in common as human beings and where we stand now in our evolutionary march toward human perfection. Thus, the purpose of our story is also to understand the roots of mystical thought and how incorporating a sense of spirituality into our revolution will provide important solutions to our common dilemma.

In Volume I of Book 1, which follows, we will begin our journey with a look at the age of the matriarchy during which time, the clan mothers led us out of animality and, in so doing, came to play the primary role in defining early human society. During this long stretch of time, our idea of god evolved from nature spirits and eventually manifested as the Great Goddess, who was the supreme source of life's fertility. We will look at the social structure under matriarchy and how the roles of women and men differed from today. We will look at the worldview created by women and how that gave rise to the ancient agricultural civilizations of the world. We will look at the internal contradiction in the matriarchal system and how it led to the emergence of patriarchy, with the dawn of the father-family, private property and the state. Finally, we will look at the life of Shiva and how he developed the Tantra philosophy of the Indus Valley civilization into a mystical science which led to the idea that through certain spiritual practices one could develop a personal relationship with Divine Consciousness.

In subsequent volumes we will look at our world under patriarchy. Volume II will explore the rise of patriarchy under the warrior empires of the Middle East, northern Africa and southern Europe. In this volume, we will look at how our perception of God evolved from the Great Goddess to having pantheons of multiple gods and goddesses, to the rise of Zoroastrianism who proposed only one good and one bad god. We will see the birth of monotheism in the West with the Jewish priests. We will look at how Jewish mysticism gave rise to Jesus Christ and the Christian mysticism and Islamic mysticism that followed. We will also see how the position of women gradually degraded from being leaders of society to being mere private property of men.

Volume III will explore the Middle Ages in Europe beginning with the fall of Rome and the rise of the barbarian states. We will observe how the Catholic Church gained and maintained its administrative power over all of Western Europe and how the priests created mind-stultifying dogmas that came to replace the mystical teachings of their spiritual master, Jesus Christ. We will look at the Crusades, the Inquisitions and the Witch Hunts which further degraded women under Church rule.

Volume IV looks at the birth of Modern History with the decline of the Church's power and the rise of secular intellectual thought. We will witness the hundred years of war between the Catholics and Protestants for religious dominance. In this struggle, we will see how freedom of thought led to secular philosophy and how human reason (science) came to challenge the blind faith of religion. Finally, we will look at the emergence of the capitalist class and its partnership with Protestantism. We will witness the expansion of this materialist philosophy in the quest for national empire building, and the devastating impact that colonialism and slavery had on the world's non-white populations. This volume also looks at the early history of the United States as it evolved to become the greatest capitalist nation in the world.

In Volume V (the final volume) on Contemporary History, we will explore the history of the United States from the end of WWII at which time it gained the status of a global empire. We will go backstage to observe how the US capitalist ruling class made its plans for world conquest and how their designs are being carried out each day by politicians regardless of party affiliation. Under these conditions we will witness the impact of the ruling class' plans on the American people and our struggle to make ends meet. We will see how the lust for wealth has led us, and our planet, to the brink of disaster.

In Book 2, we look at the subject of Universal Ideology and why current religious and political ideologies are insufficient to help us address the global problems that confront humanity today. We will unpack the components of a Universal Ideology, including an analysis of social psychologies, human nature, spirituality, economics and politics.

In Book 3 of this trilogy, we will explore the need for Revolution and envision how a universal ideology can help us manifest our individual and collective power to transform society for the betterment of all. We will define a Nuclear Revolution and the requirements for it to occur. We will examine how it will impact all aspects of human endeavor, including personal, interpersonal, cultural, political, economic and environmental relations.

# Matriarchy, the Goddess and Her Consort

LONG BEFORE HUMAN BEINGS learned to express their thoughts in writing, women governed society. The warring states of men did not yet exist. The matriarchy period stretched from the dawn of our species in Africa, around 2.5 million years ago, to the time the first Aryan patriarchal tribes came crashing out of the Caucasus Mountains and descended onto the fertile plains of the Indus Valley, as recently as ten thousand years ago. For hundreds of years, the books and papers of historians and other academics, and the scriptures and dogmas written by the priests of patriarchal religions have long ignored or denied the existence of the matriarchy, which obfuscates the contribution of women to human evolution. They could not believe, or perhaps refused to believe, that women ever governed human society. Who could possibly think that women ever stood superior to men! Yet, the simple truth is that as long as we remain blinded by the myth of male superiority and female inferiority, we will not be unable to create a better world for our children and grandchildren. It will not be an easy task to change the world because the myth of uninterrupted male superiority is now so deeply encoded in the subconscious programming of modern society. The myth has made us mentally ill, and, like most mentally ill people, we live in a state of constant denial concerning the seriousness of our disease.

The myth of eternal male superiority and eternal female inferiority stands against the very laws of motion. In a world where everything is constantly changing, it is impossible to have a contradiction composed of two poles that remain infinitely distinct and separate. Movement consists of an interpenetration of opposites. Yet, men in power remain sentimentally attached to their mythology and will do everything in their power, including the use of brute force, to keep women subservient. This distorted perception, backed by brute force, prevents our society from progressing and stunts our growth as human beings. In order to progress as individuals and as a human society, we must now begin to break down this myth. To do so, it is necessary to know that there was a time in human history when women governed human society and God was a woman, more precisely, a black woman. While this story contradicts all the myths of patriarchal society, nonetheless it is true. Let us now explore what recent discoveries have taught us about the roles of men and women during the development of Western Civilization.

## The Time of the Matriarchy

Scientists place the origins of our genus (homo) about 2.5 million years ago and the origin of our species (sapiens) about two hundred thousand years ago.[4] The oldest discovered human skulls found in Africa are dated about one hundred and sixty thousand years ago.[5] Around fifty thousand years ago, we were already modern human beings having language, tools, trade, science and pursuing other cultural developments.[6] Written history, by contrast, only began about five thousand years ago.

It was the females of our species, in their role as mothers, who ushered us out of animality and into humanity. Therefore, we can say that the matriarchy, however primitive, originated about 2.5 million years ago. This corresponds roughly to the beginning of the Paleolithic Age, when humans first started using stone artifacts, and covers roughly ninety-five percent[7] of human prehistory. For this reason, the Paleolithic Age is also called the Stone Age.

The earliest undisputed evidence of artistic expression during the Paleolithic Age comes in the form of bracelets, beads, and small female figurines found at sites such as the Blombos Cave.[8] The *Venus of Willendorf*, a statuette of a female figure with ample breasts and a clearly defined vulva, is estimated to have been made between twenty-eight and twenty-five years ago. In addition to having performed religious ceremonies in caves, humans had already begun to take part in long distance trade for rare commodities like ochre, an earth pigment used for body painting during religious rituals.[9]

For hundreds of thousands of years, our species spent the majority of time hunting, gathering, and scavenging. By around one hundred and sixty-four thousand years ago, modern humans were collecting and cooking shellfish. By ninety thousand years ago, they were making special fishing tools. Human fossil remains in Israel date to about this time.

We can estimate that the golden age of matriarchy began in earnest toward the end of the Mid-Paleolithic Age and the onset of the Upper Pleistocene Age about fifty thousand years ago and lasted to about ten thousand years ago with the dawn of patriarchy.

The Pleistocene Age, which began about seventy thousand years ago was subject to wide temperature swings due to the advance and retreat of the glaciers during the ice ages. In the retreat of the glaciers, around fifty thousand years ago, a huge migration of animals and humans pushed out of Africa into Eurasia. By forty-five thousand years ago, humans lived at sixty-one degrees north latitude in Europe (Norway and Sweden).[10] By thirty-two thousand years ago, Japan was reached, and by twenty-nine thousand, Siberia above the Arctic Circle was inhabited.[11]

The populations in Africa moved north in waves, and in doing so developed the survival skills necessary to move from the tropics of Africa to the cooler temperatures of the middle latitudes.[12] Groups of these Mediterranean people, who were predominantly hunters, followed the deer and other animals further north as the glaciers melted.[13] They eventually made their way up into the Caucasian Mountains to present-day central Russian. These hunting tribes became known as the Nordic Aryans.

About seven thousand years ago, these nomadic Aryan tribes began to sweep south into the Middle East, west into northern Europe, and east into India, where their chariot riding armies swept over the matriarchal agricultural civilization of the Indus Valley. The meeting of these white, patriarchal warriors with the indigenous, brown, matriarchal Dravidians, who were farmers and mystics, created a clash of cultures that continues to reverberate in the subconscious of the human species even today. The interpenetration of these opposing cultures gave rise to the Indo-European civilization that provided the base for the development of Western Civilization. As such, this clash of cultures set the course of our present subconscious programming regarding gender and race relations, as well as our concept of God. The hardy Aryans abandoned the cold and severe climate of the Caucasus to settle in the more hospitable garden lands of India. At the time of their arrival, the Indus Valley was governed by one of the most sophisticated matriarchal civilization to ever exist on the planet.

Let us begin our presentation of the matriarchy by looking at the earliest days of the female-governed clan and the environmental conditions from which it arose.

During the transition of the human clan out of the hominid primal horde, the women, in their role as mothers, who established the rules regarding human relationships. Their authority developed naturally out of the mothers' role of caregiver. During the primate and hominid stages of development, the mothers, in cooperation with each other, protected the young and developed communication methods (eye signals, vocal sounds, body postures, etc.) to teach them the skills necessary to survive in the group. Except for the alpha male, who had sexual access to females, adult males were peripheral to the group structure. This behavior on the part of the mothers existed around 2.5 million years ago and continued to exist up until the beginning of patriarchy some ten thousand years ago.

In 1930, H. L. Mencken wrote the following in his *Treatise on the Gods*:

> "Primitive society, like many savage societies of our own time, was probably strictly matriarchal. The mother was the head of the family. ...What masculine authority there was resided in the mother's brother. He was the man of the family, and to him the children yielded respect and obedience. Their father, at best, was simply a pleasant friend who fed them and played with them; at worst, he was an indecent loafer who sponged on the mother. They belonged, not to his family, but to their mother's. As they grew up they joined their uncle's group of hunters, not their father's. This matriarchal organization of the primitive tribe, though it finds obvious evidential support in the habits of higher animals, has been questioned by many anthropologists, but of late one of them, Briffault, demonstrated its high probability in three immense volumes [*The Mothers: A Study of the Origins of Sentiments and Institutions*]. It is hard to escape the cogency of his arguments, for they are based upon an almost overwhelming accumulation of facts.... Thus it appears that man, in his remote infancy, was by no means the lord of creation that he has since become."[14]

Briffault is known for what is called Briffault's Law: "The female, not the male, determines all the conditions of the animal family. Where the female can derive no benefit from association with the male, no such association takes place."[15]

The existence of matriarchy is now well established, regardless of the great investment that male-dominated organizations have made historically to deny its existence. But, the fact that it existed thousands of years before the creation of written language around six thousand years ago,[16] has made it difficult to piece together the story of its evolution and transformation. Yet, the story has been verified in a number of ways, including observing the current behaviors and rituals of primates and primitive tribes; examining ancient architecture, scrolls, myths, and stories; and understanding the development of certain words across languages. Today, there are many books on the subject of matriarchy; for example, *When God Was a Woman, When God Was a Black Woman, The White Goddess, The Mothers, The Language of the Goddess*, etc. Among these books, Evelyn Reed's, "*Woman's Evolution: From Matriarchal Clan to Patriarchal Family*, presents the clearest picture of life in matriarchal society and how mother-rule changed to brother-rule and finally into father-rule.[17] It is fair to say that Reed's book has provided humanity with an understanding of gender relations comparable to Marx's contribution to our understanding of class relations. It is a profound piece of work.

We will now attempt to tell the story of matriarchy, which can only be a sketchy summary of a time that was exceedingly long and complex.

## The Clan

To evolve out of the primal hordes of the primates and hominids into the human clan structure, the mothers had to establish certain rules. Their main concern was keeping peace within the clan, usually a group around twenty-five individuals. The earliest of these rules consisted of two taboos. Firstly, it was forbidden for males to eat anyone in their group, and secondly, it was forbidden for males to have sex with any female in the group. These taboos were essential to maintaining the stability of day-to-day clan existence. Through these rules the females taught the males (their brothers) and their young that the clan was a special group. Essentially, the taboos said we are the *human beings* and we protect each other. As the human groups became more complex, ceremonies were created to officially make the males officially into human beings. Because the males could not have sex with anyone in the clan, it was necessary to make raids on other clans to have sex. This created a great disturbance among all the clans. To solve this problem the women created *clan confederations*. Clan confederations created peace between the men of local clans, but having sex with females within the clan confederation was still taboo. Thus, such confederations only created greater fear and violence among the men, who now had to travel greater distances to have sex with females. Eventually, the mothers developed the tribal system. A tribe is composed of two clan confederations. With the innovation of the tribe, males and females from one confederation could now have sex with those of the other confederation. This significant development in social formations created greater peace and harmony among tribal members. It made possible the transition to small villages and agriculture. By the time the mothers had established an agricultural civilization, perhaps as early twelve thousand years ago, or earlier, they had already taken the clan system through the evolutions of clan confederations, tribes, and nations. By the time matriarchy reached its golden age, the great agricultural civilizations were in existence. The mothers had also developed mathematics, astrology/astronomy, medicine, extensive trade routes, and developed the technology to produce a wide variety of foods, tools, pottery, jewelry, weapons, textiles, and other goods. Some tribes had even begun to heat and work metals. Of greater significance, the women had developed the first comprehensive idea of divinity and the religious practices needed to unite themselves with the intentions of their divinity. They called her the Great Goddess. The idea of the Great Goddess arose from African tribes and thus was a black female divinity. In her book, *Yurugu: An African-Centered Critique of European Cultural Thought and Behavior*, Marimba Ani tells us, "In the ancient religious traditions of Africa and other parts of the world, we find again and again the predominance of the mother goddess; the valorization of the female principle, the earth symbol. These traditions were well developed before it was possible to speak of a "Western" or "Western European peoples."[18]

During the golden age of matriarchy, women moved freely as warriors, traders, ambassadors, and priestesses. In their role as priestesses, they evolved the knowledge of the natural cycles, including the lunar and solar calendars. They attributed control of these cycles to the Great Goddess, who changed her form according to the seasons. In the spring She was the Virgin, in the summer and fall, the Mother, and in the late fall and winter, the Crone. The concept of the Great Goddess evolved from the need to understand the annual agricultural cycle of life and death and the need to ensure that the fertility of the land was sufficient to feed the people each year. During this period of mother-rule, human beings developed first great agricultural civilizations of Egypt, Mesopotamia, and the Indus Valley. The people believed that these great civilizations existed by virtue of the grace and bounty of the Great Goddess.

During the matriarchy, all religious rituals centered on the mystery of life and death. Just as the crops were born each spring, the mothers had the ability to bring life into existence out of their own bodies. The knowledge related to this mysterious act made them magical. With the development of their religion, based upon the giving of life, they became more than women or mothers. They had become goddesses. As goddesses, they could control what happened on this earth.

## The Moon and the Mystery of Motherhood

Since the dawn of human consciousness, the central mystery for women had been the act of creating human life within themselves. The fact that a woman could produce another life out of her own body has always been central to the worldview of women. Solving the mystery of how this happens and how all life happens was the central preoccupation of the matriarchy.

By exploring the cause of human birth, initially women all over the world came to believe that pregnancy resulted from a particular union of a woman's blood with a *spirit*. No one at the time had any idea men's sperm had a role in the creation of a child. Primitive people found themselves surrounded by life forms that they believed had similar intelligence to them and were capable of anything. Every rock, plant, tree, animal, etc., had a spirit or life force within it, and these spirits could be benevolent or malevolent at any moment. In fact, Julian Jaynes, the author of *The Origins of Consciousness in the Breakdown of the Bicameral Mind*, informs us that even the voices that women and men heard in their minds were not yet attributed to themselves but to outside spirits.[19] The voice of the spirit in one's mind could be from an animal or plant, a dead ancestor, or eventually a goddess or god. It did not matter. Spirits could take any form they chose.

If a spirit did not enter her body and coagulate her blood, a woman did not become pregnant. Instead, her life's blood flowed out of her body. Why did a woman bleed from her vagina every so many days? There had to be a profound reason for this. The women discovered that the moon was responsible for this. They observed that every night the moon arose out of the earth and every morning it descended back into it. They also noticed that it changed its form in a cyclical manner. It grew from nothing into a full moon and then gradually waned again into nothing. Women noticed that the flow of their menstrual blood corresponded to a particular phase of the moon. One complete cycle of the moon, the women called a month. Every month they bled. When they did not bleed they were with child and their blood was being converted into life.

Therefore, women believed that the moon produced and controlled their life's blood. They called the moon a goddess. She was the controller of life. In this way, women concluded that all life came about as the result of a union between the goddess and a spirit (totem). The Moon Goddess is still worshipped in Zimbabwe as Bomo Rambi, in Ghana as Buruku, in Benin as Gleti, in West Africa as Mawu, and by many other names throughout Africa.[20]

In time, women came to understand that the moon was not the sole controller of life; rather the moon was a part of the earth. It rose out of the earth and it descended into the earth. The earth itself was the goddess. They called her Mother Earth, which has many names depending upon the culture. The Greeks, for example, called her Gaia; Indians called her Durga; and in the Congo they called her Nzambi.

Women came to correlate their own wombs with the caves of Mother Earth. They believed that the mystery of life on earth could be understood, and even controlled, by understanding the mystery of these caves. They believed that the processes activated within the womb of Mother Earth caused life to be born on the surface. Not only the birth of life, but also the activities of life were determined in the caves of Mother Earth. If the women could solve the secret of the caves, they could also control life on the surface. With such thoughts, the women developed rituals, which they called magic, to gain control of the secrets of Mother Earth. Herein resides the meaning of cave art. It was not men who created cave art; it was the women who created it in their attempt to understand and control the activities of life. Cave art was a symbolic expression, created to influence the clan's daily life. The ability to have a successful hunt or to have successful relationships with other clans, with the life forms that fed them or wished them evil, with the Goddess, or with each other were influenced by the mothers' pictures on the walls of caves.

To the ancient matriarchs, the caves held the deepest mysteries. Throughout the entire known world, early goddess worship took place in caves.

## The Great Goddess

In India, a place with one of the most ancient matriarchal societies, the oldest form of the Dravidian goddess was Kurukulla, the "Mother of Caverns."[21] Kurukulla was colored red like the moon. Later she became an expression of Kali, the Great Goddess, who was worshipped in cave temple complexes like Ellora, Ajanta, and Elephanta.

This same goddess was known as Rhea on the Isle of Crete. She was the daughter of Gaia, the Earth Goddess, and was called the "mother of gods." All life arose from her uterine cave on Mount Dicte. Much later, men would say that Zeus, the father of the Gods, was given birth by the Goddess Rhea in this cave.[22] The study of cave rituals leads us to believe that the first queens became anointed as representatives of the Goddess and spoke the words of the Goddess. Gods were born in the womb of the Great Goddess. Even today, we have words like *dictate* and *edict* because of pronouncements of the goddess's holy laws that were derived from Mount Dicte.

The ancient Persians (the Phyrigians)) worshiped Cybele, the "Cave Dweller," who was the Great Mother of the Gods. Cybele became Sibyl when she was brought to Rome as late as 204 BC.

The Europeans worshiped the Great Goddess as Mother Hel. Holland derives its names from her, so also does the Christian concept of hell. The early "hell" seems to have been a uterine cave shrine or cave of rebirth known as *hellir*.

Caves, in addition to controlling life on earth, were also entrances to the underworld. Caves were wombs, but they were also tombs, the place of death. The Goddess, worshipped as the Nether Moon, was called Nehellenia.[23] In the deepest place in the underworld she was the "eater of the dead." Another mystery of caves that had to be solved was how it was possible for life to be regenerated in the underworld, the realm of the dead. Each spring, new energy came out of the earth to create new vegetation and baby animals. How did this happen?

By probing the depths of caves, the mothers hoped to find the place where the sun and the moon resided when they were not in the heavens. Did the moon die each day? Did the sun die each night? What was the relation between life and death? The search for the meaning of the cycles of the moon and the sun, and the answer to related questions, gave rise to human abstract thought as well as the first thoughts regarding divinity. Such thinking evolved through stages. Even though the voices of the spirits and deities were heard inside the mind, they were conceptualized as external forces. Early humans worshipped ancestors because they could still hear their voices even after they had died. They worshipped ghosts, animal and plant totems (spirits), nature goddesses and gods, and finally the spirit of all life, the Great Goddess.

Sometime around twelve thousand years ago, the mothers made the transition from hunting and gathering to agricultural production, and they began to reorganize the environment to meet their needs. They discovered, through their understanding of the Goddess's magic in caves, that they also could perform magic rituals by which they could control the growth and breeding of plants and animals. This discovery led to farming and animal husbandry. As the mothers invested more time in producing food, they created more wealth and more security. Small clans expanded in size to clan confederations, tribes, and, eventually, nations composed of many tribes. In time, small farming villages became towns, and towns became walled cities. With more food available, the human population began to increase dramatically. As surplus was created, the distribution of the surplus and the protection of it came into question. This led eventually to an increased role for males in society.

It is uncertain exactly when the idea of the Great Goddess arose in the human mind, but it most likely happened in Africa. Even today people in Africa worship the Great Goddess in the form of Ala, Ale, Ane, Asase, Yaa, Aberewa, Efua, Chineke, etc.[24] Before the arrival of the Aryans in India, the Great Goddess was called

Tara. When worshiping Tara, the people believed that, "all you see is Her body, made of green light, all you hear is Her divine speech, and all your thoughts as Her divine wisdom. Every molecule of air is Her divine energy and when you lie down, your head rests in Her lap."[25]

The Great Goddess was the answer to the questions about birth, nurturance, and death in the annual cycle. Because of her, all of life was born, sustained, and died. Because of her, the agricultural harvest was successful or not. The mothers made up stories about how the Great Goddess controlled the life cycle. These stories constituted our earliest myths, and rituals were created to communicate their significance to the people. Each fall after the harvest, the Crone would spread death on the land. She would then descend into the underworld where, on the winter solstice, she was born again as the Virgin. Each spring the Virgin gave birth to life anew. Once life was established, the Virgin would change into the Mother and she would nurture life until the harvest. Then she would again become the Crone who brought winter to the land. Finally, she would arise again in the spring as the Virgin. Thus, the Great Goddess had three aspects, birth, nurturance, and death/reincarnation, each fulfilling a certain role in the annual cycle of life.

The Dravidians created the Indus Valley agricultural civilization and called their goddess Kala-Nath, the "Womb of Creation."[26] Kala-nath became the Great Goddess who represented the power to give life, sustain life, and destroy life in her roles as Virgin, Mother, and Crone.[27]

As the Aryans merged with the Dravidians to give rise to the Indo-European civilization, the idea of Kala-Nath as the Great Goddess spread westward. Some people took the first part of Kala-Nath and called their goddess Kali; the Irish called her Kelle; the Saxons called her Kale; and the Finnish called her Kalma, Kauri, Kore, Ker, Car, Q're, Ceres, etc. Words derived from this name for the Goddess are *kernel, cardiac,* and *core.* Other people named their goddesses based on Nath. For example, the Sumerians called her Anna-Nin or Inanna. The Canaanites, Amorites, Hebrews, and other mid-eastern tribes called her Anath or Anerth. The Phoenicians in Cyprus called her Anat. The Egyptians called her Anerth. The Phrygians called her Nana, mother of the Savior. The Celts in Europe called her Ana or Anu. Di-ana or Di-nah was also a European name meaning Goddess Ana. The Scandinavian tribes called her Nanna. The Romans called her "Eternal Anna." Even the Christian priests, in order to legitimize Jesus Christ to the common people, contended that his grandmother was St. Anne.[28]

The Great Goddess was held in the same high esteem as God the Father is held today. The Sumerian prayer declared, "Hear O you regions, the praise of Queen Nana; magnify the Creatress, exalt the dignified, exalt the Glorious One, draw nigh unto the Mighty Lady."[29]

## The Virgin and the Serpent

We have said that the Great Goddess had three aspects, the Virgin who created life, the Mother who sustained life, and the Crone who destroyed life. How did the goddess in the form of the Virgin create all life? The most ancient creation myths involved an interaction between the Virgin and a serpent.

The Virgin aspect of the Goddess was often imagined as a beautiful garden, lush with life. Our word *paradise*, for example, derives from the Persian Pairidaeza, which was "a garden surrounding the holy mountain of the gods, where the Tree of Life bore the fruit of immortality."[30] Pairidaeza was also the divine Virgin who would give birth to the future Redeemer.

The word for the Garden of Eden in Hebrew was *pardes* and was derived from the same Virgin Paradise. However, we are getting ahead of ourselves because these are patriarchal myths, which were later grafted onto historic matriarchal images of the Goddess.

Let us go back to the earliest days when the mothers were beginning their descent into the caves of the earth seeking answers to life's fundamental questions. What did they find in those caves? In many instances, they discovered strange and awesome caverns with rivers running through them. They found beautiful precious stones and gleaming metals. They discovered weird nocturnal animals and insects. They found the roots of mighty trees and the bones of the dead. Undoubtedly, one of the most intriguing discoveries within the caves was the muscular serpents that slithered in and out of the shadows. Aside from the sexual energy they generated, the serpents were also considered magical because they could shed their skins. It was a general belief in the ancient world that snakes did not die like other animals, but by the shedding of their skins, they would emerge reborn into a new life.[31] They were immortal.

In the most ancient myths, the immortal serpent was originally identified with the Goddess herself. The serpent, as the totemic form of the Goddess, was able to give immortality to all life. "The Indian Serpent Goddess Kadru gave birth to all the Nagas (cobra people) and made them immortal by feeding them her divine lunar blood."[32] In India today, the Nagas are still considered nature spirits and the protectors of springs, wells, and rivers. The Nagas remain objects of great reverence in some parts of South India where women still gather at Hindu temples to worship the Nāgas that are carved in stones. They are considered female snake goddesses and are believed to make women fertile, to protect the women and their families, and to bring prosperity.[33]

Later, "Hinduism's Ananta the Infinite was the serpent mother who embraced Vishnu and other gods during their dead phase."[34] As women's spiritual knowledge increased, the goddess became known as Kundalini; she was the soul in serpent form coiled at the base of the spine and induced, through Tantric practices, to arise through the spinal chakras toward the head, bringing self-realization and eternal enlightenment.

The Cambodians had a serpent Goddess whom they worshipped in the temple of Angkor Wat.[35]

The Negritos called the serpent Goddess Mat Chinoi, who was the mother of the Chinese people. They believe that beautiful angels lived in her womb and welcomed the dead. Her womb was considered to be paradise.

The Babylonians worshipped the Goddess Kadi of Der as a serpent who had a woman's head and breasts. Like the Babylonians, the Acadians worshiped Ninhursag, "She who gives life to the dead." She was also called "Mistress of Serpents."[36]

The ancient Agean world primarily worshiped women and snakes. Egyptians also believed that the snake was a totemic form of the Goddess and held magical wisdom. Egypt's archaic Mother of Creation was the serpent Per-Uatchet or Buto. The hieroglyphic *uraeus* (i.e., snake) was a sign for the Goddess.

After some time, the serpent came to represent, not the Goddess, but her consort. Perhaps this invention was due to the decision of the queens who now had another purpose for the serpent. Women now came to believe that the first onset of menstruation must be caused by copulation with the supernatural snake. Not yet aware of fatherhood, they supposed that this snake also rendered each woman fertile and helped her to conceive.

If the moon was the source of menstrual blood, the snake was responsible for coagulating this blood into form. Therefore, the ancient belief that human life was a result of a woman meeting with the totem spirit had its philosophical substantiation in the belief that the Goddess mated with this Serpent to produce all life.

In this way, the idea of a male deity arose in the minds of the people. The first male deities, like Nahusha in the Vedas and Nehushtan in the Old Testament, were serpent gods. In order for Indra, the Aryan God of War, to replace the Goddess and establish male authority, he had to fight a great battle against Vitra, the Serpent consort of the Goddess, who held back the waters and caused a drought.[37] Holding back the waters was a symbolic way of saying that the Goddess and her consort controlled the mysteries of life.

As the male serpent deity became the phallic consort of the Goddess, he often became a "father" of races because he was the

Mother's original mate. In some myths, he was no more than a living phallus that she created for her own sexual pleasure. In other myths, he took part in the work of creation. Let it be said for now that the union of the Goddess and the Serpent in matriarchal creation myths was a universal phenomenon.

However, giving birth was not the only role of the Goddess. Having given birth, she also had the responsibility to nurture life and, in the end, to destroy it. Yet, this destruction was not eternal. The Goddess destroyed only to give birth again in a new form each spring. In the mothers' way of thinking nothing died eternally, only its present form died. Like the sun died each night and was reborn each day, so all of life died and was reborn. As the animals died and were reborn again in new forms and as the plants died each winter and were reborn each spring, so too did humans die and were also reborn. Sometimes they were reborn as gods or goddesses, sometimes as plants or animals, and sometimes as humans again. The living consciousness that inhabited forms did not die, but only took new forms.

The examination of the roles of the Goddess as virgin, mother, and crone, over time, brought into play a more complex understanding of reality and more complex ritual practices. The discovery of the *life cycle* constituted the deepest of magical knowledge. What followed, due to this discovery, were the rituals of blood; the creation of sacred things; orgiastic rituals and human sacrifices; and the making of gods, saviors, and scapegoats.

## Blood Sacrifice

The mothers believed that their own bodies were the microcosms that mirrored the process by which the Goddess produced and controlled life on earth. They were tied to the Goddess through the flow of their blood.

It was blood, therefore, that created the greatest mystery, that established the greatest bond, and that was the central element in all ritual performances. Blood was the gift of the Goddess to all women and through women to all life. The women had already been using ochre as a symbolic substance. Perhaps by now they understood ocher to be the blood of the soil itself. If blood was a gift, it was also a sacrifice. Mothers gave their blood to their children in the womb or returned it to the Goddess each month. This was the demand of the Goddess. She gave blood and she took blood. She gave life and she took life.

At first, the mothers offered their own menstrual blood to the Goddess. Under certain circumstances, however, the mothers came to believe that their own menstrual blood was not enough to appease Her or to induce Her to create a bountiful harvest, or a larger herd, or more young in the tribe. They had to give more in order to receive more. In this way, the mothers came to offer the blood of others to the Goddess.

## The Sacred King

The mothers began to designate certain young males for sacrifice. *Sacrifice* and *sacred* have the same root word, *sacer*, which means "untouchable." Just as menstruating women were considered *sacer*, so chosen men now became *sacer* because they were a part of the same mystery. A sacer person or thing was set aside for a divine purpose—consumption by a divinity. The sacrificial victims, whether human or animal, were almost invariably male. Males were expendable because they had no role in giving life. It is clear that male blood was sacrificed on the earliest religious altars and offered to the Goddess.

In some tribes, the blood of the man or animal was ingested by the mothers or spurted on their vaginas in the belief that it would beget a human offspring. The belief was, "Whatever is killed becomes father."[38] Because sacrifices were males, the totemic animal ancestors were usually paternal as well. For example, if a wolf was killed in sacrifice and the women became pregnant their children would become members of the Wolf clan. It is said that Romulus and Remus, the founders of Rome, were raised by a wolf.[39] In becoming a sacrifice to the Goddess, an animal gained human status. A human sacrifice, on the other hand, merited the stature of a god. Let us see how this occurred.

As clans grew into tribes and tribes into tribal alliances or nations, politics became more complex. It became necessary to centralize power into the hands of an individual. The person the mothers chose for this role was called the queen. In the earliest times, women viewed her as the most resourceful, powerful, and beautiful one. The Queen became the embodiment of the Great Goddess herself. She was worshiped by the all people as the Goddess and later as the Mother of the gods. With the creation of the role of queen, the ancient ritual of blood sacrifice produced a new kind of offering to the Goddess—the *sacred king*.

In the beginning, all kings were *sacred*. They did not come to power by virtue of their own might or by inheriting a crown from their father; instead, they were chosen by the Queen to serve a sacred purpose.

Marriage to the Queen was essential to the position of kingship. Ashurbanipal said he ruled by the grace of the Goddess Ishtar; he was the king "whom her hands created." Shamash-shum-ukin of Babylon said he was chosen for kingship by the same Goddess under her title of Erua, Queen of the Gods. King Esarkaddon of Assyria said he was "the beloved of Queen Ishtar, the Goddess of everything, the unsparing weapon, who brings destruction to the land of the enemy." Ishme-Dagan, King of Isin in 1860 BC, said he was "he who Inanna, Queen of Heaven and Earth has chosen for her beloved husband."[40]

While these kings were ruling kings, who existed after the transition from matriarchy to patriarchy, they kings still saw themselves as chosen by the Great Goddess. But we are getting ahead of ourselves.

In the days of the Queen's power, her choice of her king largely depended upon the candidate's sex appeal or, more precisely, his sexual capacity. It also depended upon his courage in the face of death. The Sanskrit word for manliness was *Vir*. It is the root of *virility* as well as *virtue* and in time *virulent*. The queen's sexual acceptance of the king was important for the entire tribe because his lovemaking and the quality of his death determined the fertility of the land and even the lives of the people themselves. This did not imply, however, that the Queen believed that the King's sperm was responsible for her pregnancy. It meant only that good lovemaking gave strength and pleasure to the Queen and, through her, life and energy for her people. Through the quality of the king's death, the sacrifice of his blood and his flesh were returned to the people and the earth through an offering to the Great Goddess. The Goddess's acceptance of it was the real test of the king's virtue as far as the people were concerned. If the harvest was great and if the herds multiplied, then the Goddess was pleased by the sacrifice of the king. In many myths, a sacred king became a star in the heavens and took his place among the deities for all time.

Among certain tribes, the Queen chose the king after a test of merit. Often, however, it depended more upon whom the Queen favored. The length of the king's reign was often based on the whimsy of the Queen. In more structured societies, it was predetermined. It was believed that the Goddess "needed the refreshment of a new lover at stated intervals."[41]

> "Up to AD 1810, kings of Zimbabwe were ceremonially strangled to death by their wives at the moon temple every four years. Kings of ancient Thebes reigned for seven years, so did Kings of Canaan. Myths suggest a similar seven-year period for each king of Crete. Cretan Kings were never allowed to grow old; they always died in the full bloom of youth"[42]

The killing of the king, in most instances, was significantly more than the Queen tiring of an old lover. It was a ritual steeped in the tradition of blood sacrifice. The king's flesh and blood was very sacred to the Goddess. As such, it had many uses. It was scattered on the earth to feed the plants and animals; it was eaten by the priestesses or by the people to make them strong; and it was used to bathe the images of the Goddess.

Certain tribes found the Goddess more blood thirsty than others. For them, neither menstrual blood nor the king's blood would appease Her. Hundreds of men might be sacrificed to Anath in a single ritual. Although the political reasons for such slaughters are unknown, history testifies to their reality. The Ras Shamra texts, which reveal Canaanite practices; for example, describe the sacrificial rites to Anath, who was fertilized by the blood of men: "Violently she smites and gloats, Anath cuts them down and gazes; her liver exults in mirth... For she plunges her knees in the blood of the soldiers, her loins in the gore of the warriors, till she has had her fill of slaughtering in the house, of cleaving among the tables."[43]

Such massacre we might easily attribute to the male of the species, but could women have been as blood thirsty? The Ras Shamra texts, which paint a picture of a blood thirsty Great Goddess, do not go back to the matriarchal period. The texts, which were discovered in Syria, are from a period that scientists believed was from 1600 BC to 1200 BC.[44] This is thousands of years after patriarchy began. As such, it appears that even while Semitic kings continued to worship the Goddess Anath, their penchant for violence was much greater than that of the earlier women priestesses. The Goddess became much more violent and blood thirsty within the patriarchy. Anath hung the shorn penises of her victims on her goatskin apron or *aegis*. In other myths, we have the "Lady of the Serpent Skirt" who made new life from Quetzalcoatl's genital blood and Athena, who wore "serpents" on her aegis.

Ritual slaughter was not initially so gratuitous. It was based on the understanding that women had concerning the process of life and death.

Out of the long tradition of blood rituals as related to the life cycle, the idea of the Savior or the Messiah evolved. The sacred king became the Savior or the Messiah. The women had discovered the cycle of the day, of the week, and of the month. In time, they discovered an even larger cycle. Through exact mathematical calculations, the priestesses created the lunar *calendar* (named after Kala-Nath). Every thirteen months, each comprised of twenty-eight days, a new cycle could be discerned. This was the year. The discovery of the year was of immense importance. With the understanding of this cycle, women could chart the birth and death of all life forms. They could make preparations for winter. They could time their activity. They could judge the lifespan of species. The application of this knowledge was profound. Agriculture, for example, would have been impossible without this knowledge. With it, the mothers were able to create the first human civilization built on agriculture.

Thus, we can see how the knowledge of cycles, and cycles within cycles, proved invaluable to ancient societies, and how the rituals of magic became so deeply rooted in human consciousness. In India, the priestesses called the annual cycle the wheel of karma. The Greeks called it the wheel of rebirth; the Romans called it the wheel of fortune.

The understanding of cycles also brought with it the idea of reincarnation, which means "re-fleshing." It was an obvious idea that emerged from mother-wisdom concerning the cycle of birth, death, and rebirth.

To bring the earth back to life each spring required a very special knowledge, a very special ritual, and a very special magic. By fifteen thousand years ago, the priestesses were well acquainted with the movement of the astral bodies. They had already evolved the basic knowledge of astronomy/astrology and mathematics. An archaic term for astrology was *mathesis*, literally, mother-wisdom. The most well known astrologers, the Chaldeans, were known as *mathematici* (i.e., learned mothers).[45] Men were completely mystified by this early science of women. The Sanskrit *matra* was the same word for *mother* and *measurement*. The Greek word *meter* also had this double meaning. According to the *Vayu Purana* (Vedic scriptures of the Aryans composed in India) they had watched the women doing spacial and temporal calculations for so long that they believed that it was the women's mathematics that allowed them to give birth to life. Men imagined that if they could master these skills, they too could give birth to life. Male ancestors told one another that if they could only learn to measure the earth, they would "happily create progeny."[46]

As males came to play a larger role in society, the creation myth changed. A typical example of this is a story in which the Goddess had a son who had two opposing natures and that killed each other (or were killed by the Goddess) and were given rebirth in an endless yearly cycle. For example, according to the Canaanite priestesses, Anath had a son Mot/Aleyin. Each fall, Anath cast her death curse (*anathema*) on Mot, who then became the Lord of Death and went to the lowest point in the underworld to rule. Mot represented the castrated, sterile aspect of the fertile Aleyin.

In a sacred drama, which occurred each fall, Anath broke Mot's reed scepter signifying his castration. She then slew him and used his blood to refresh the soil for next year's crop. "She seizes Mot, the sun divine. With her sickle she cleaves him. With her flail she beats him." Each spring, Anath would wed Aleyin anew and the Earth would again become fertile.

This story was acted out in the ritual of the sacred king. A sacred king would be slain each fall and another recreated each spring to represent the death of Mot and the life of Aleyin.

Many myths, which contain stories of a son killing his father or a father killing his son, must be understood within the context of the cycles of life in the role of the sacred king. Each new king entered a love-death relationship with the Goddess. In replacing the old king, the new king referred to him as *father*, and the old king referred to the new king as his *son*. In myths expressing the annual cycle of life and death, the son would kill the father each spring, and the father, in turn, would kill the son each fall. In this context, also, all sacred kings were considered to be sons of god, who was the first sacred king.

The sacred king wore a king's robes, sat on a king's throne, lay with the queen, and wielded a scepter. Then, after so many days or years, he was stripped, scourged, and hanged or impaled "between heaven and earth." The object of scourging was to make the sacred king shed tears and blood for fertility magic. Upon his death, he ascended into heaven and united with the heavenly father (i.e., the original totem father or first sacrifice). Probably, the idea of resurrection into godhood induced men to accept death willingly as did the same promise induce religious saviors and martyrs in patriarchal times. This ceremony was the prototype for the idea of the Messiah or Savior during the time of patriarchy. The God, who arose from the depths of the underworld to bring new life to earth each spring and assure the people another bounty of food, was called the Savior.

As males gained more power in society and the matriarchy succumb to patriarchy, all leaders called themselves saviors, whether they were kings, holy men, generals, or emperors.

As matriarchy transitioned into patriarchy, the Sun came to represent a male God, just as the Moon had represented the Goddess.

The Lord of Death referred to the nadir of the underworld and represented the sun at its lowest aspect in the midwinter solstice. Another name was the Sun of Night. During the summer months, the tribes tended to be more loosely organized, dispersing to go hunting, exploring, food gathering, trading, etc. In the winter months, however, they tended to be more concentrated. During this period, social life tended to be much more intense. There were feasts, marriages, gift exchanges, and plenty of visiting. There was also the ritual of the Sun of Night. As astrological knowledge increased, rituals came to be performed on the solstices. Of these, the ritual of the winter solstice tended toward every excess. The Sun of Night was worshiped each winter so that he might allow the spring to come again. The most complete information concerning this activity comes to us by way of the Etruscans (early inhabitants of Italy), who called the winter sun Saturn.

> "His worship included the wearing of black clothing and the burning candles made of incense, opium, goats fat in urine, with the prayer: "Lord, whose name is august, whose power is widespread, whose spirit is sublime, oh Lord Saturn the cold, the dry, the dark, the harmful... crafty sire who knowest all wiles, who are deceitful, sage, understanding, who causest prosperity or ruin, happy or unhappy is he whom thou make us such."[47]

The worship of Saturn was called the "Saturnalia." It included the sacrifice of a sacred king, who was sent to the underworld to merge with Saturn.

In time, the killing was replaced by a symbolic killing, but the festival was never abandoned. Even in Christian times, it became a part of the midwinter Carnival. The mock execution of King Carnival was a vestige of the ancient sacrifice of the sacred king.

Another significant feature of the Saturnalia—which certainly did not make it into Christian times—was the sexual orgies, which were a part of most ancient rights, and especially the winter solstice rights. The word *orgy* comes from the Greek *orgia*, which means "secret worship."

Orgies were a fundamental part of all sacred ritual during the matriarchy. If there was death in the ancient rituals, there was also sex. Perhaps this is why our pairing of sex and violence is so deeply rooted in our collective subconscious.

The central sexual act during the matriarchal period was called, in Greek, the *hieros gamos*. It meant sacred marriage and signified the sexual union of the sacred king with the goddess in the personage of the Queen. This right was essential to the king's right to rule or to enjoy the pleasures of a god, no matter how long such tenure might prevail. But the king was also offered a spiritual reward, as the Goddess promised eternal life to those who entered her bed. The marriage of the Queen and sacred king constituted the Sacred Mystery of all ancient rights, and it became the obligation of the people to participate in this form of worship. Such activity produced an erotic and ecstatic experience, which must have had a very profound effect on the collective identity of the people as well.

It appears that orgies were a universal practice in the ancient world. Sexual rights were part of the sacred mysteries of Eleusis, Cabiria, Shaktism, early Sufism, Ophite Christianity, and many more forms of worship. It is little wonder that male-dominated patriarchal religions were so anti-sex, forcing its priests to become celibates or ascetics. It was necessary for the church to destroy human sexuality in order to destroy the matriarchy and suppress women. This suppression continues to impact us to this day. Although there is some benefit in sexual abstinence, this was certainly not the main reason that male priests denigrated women and demanded sexual countenance within the general population for millennia.

The importance of the Goddess in assuming the forms of the virgin, mother, and crone, in developing blood sacrifice, and in creating sacred kings was all related to the need of the mothers to ensure the fertility of the land so that their people would have enough food to eat each year. The fruit of this magical knowledge and rituals was the creation of an agricultural civilization that took humankind out of the Stone Age.

If we reflect upon the beliefs and rituals of the matriarchal period, we can see how powerful they were. They combined sexual behavior, the rituals of life and death, and the meaning of spirituality into a profound sentiment that captured every aspect of the human personality. Human society has not since experienced such a systematic integration of the sacred and the mundane (the material and the spiritual) in calling forth the deepest human feelings of joy, dread, and awe. It was, in fact, the women who created the Garden of Eden, the tree of life, and the tree of immortality and offered the fruits of life and immortality to humanity. It was not the serpent and the Goddess that destroyed our access to *paradise*; it was the men who destroyed the garden through constant wars and the institution of patriarchal religions. According to Barbara Walker:

> Home and mother are written over every phase of neolithic agriculture.... It was the woman who wielded the digging stick and the hoe; she who attended the garden crops and accomplished those masterpieces of selection and cross-fertilization which turned raw wild species into the prolific and richly nutritious domestic varieties: it was women who made the first containers, weaving baskets and coiling the first clay pots.... In form, the village, too, is her creation: for whatever else the village might be, it was a collective nest for the care and nurture of the young. Here she lengthened the period of childcare and playful irresponsibility, on which so much of man's higher development depends." [48]

Egyptian Scriptures emphasized the honor due "thy mother, who bore thee with much suffering. She placed thee in the Chamber of Instruction that thou mightest acquire instruction in books. She was unremitting in her care for thee, and had loaves and beer for thee in her house. When thou art grown... cast thine eyes upon her that gave thee birth and provided all good things for thee, thy mother. Let her never reproach thee."[49]

An Ethiopian woman expressed the basic psychological attitude of primitive mothers:

> "How can a man know what a woman's life is...? The man spends the night by a woman and goes away. His life and body are always the same. The woman conceives. As a

mother, she is another person from the women without child. She carries the fruit of the night nine months long in her body. Something grows into her life that never again departs from it. She is a mother. She is and remains a mother even though her child die, though all her children die. For one time she carried the child under her heart. And it does not go out of her heart ever again. Not even once it is dead. All this the man does not know; he knows nothing. He does not know the difference before love and after love, before motherhood and after motherhood. He can know nothing. Only a woman can know that and speak of that. That is why we won't be told what to do by our husbands."[50]

The Great Goddess ascended supreme throughout the whole world because she was the source of all life begot of the female. As such, she was the central figure in all religions. She was the eternal and infinite being and the creative and ruling power of heaven, earth, the underworld, and every creature and thing within them.[51]

It was the thought of the Great Goddess that inspired the women to create agriculture; to build; to weave; to make pottery; to write poetry; to make music, paintings, and drawings; to make calendars; and to invent astrology/astronomy and mathematics. Hindu scriptures say the Goddess invented alphabets, pictographs, mandalas, and other magical signs. The mothers also defined day and night, the days of the week, the month, the seasons, the year, and other units of measurement. They created Time and Death, logic and grammar. They defined nourishment, memory, victory, religious rituals; they created the Great Goddess and the idea of Divinity. Women were, therefore, the creators of the basic elements of civilization.[52]

When the white men came to America for land and wealth, many American Indians were worshiping the Goddess and were ruled by tribal chiefs elected by the Female Governesses. They surprised the

Christian missionaries with behavior more "Christian" than that of white men. A missionary said, "[W]hat is extremely surprising in men whose external appearances are wholly barbarous, is to see them treat one another with a gentleness and consideration which one does not find among common people in the most civilized countries." Indian women were known as the Life of the Nation and Mistresses of the Soil. In answer to a white questioner who could not understand the Indian reverence for women, one Indian man said, "Of course the men follow the wishes of the women; they are our mothers."[53]

As Lewis Mumford tells us:

> In the early agricultural villages of the matriarchy: "there was no ruling class to exploit the villagers, no compulsion to work for a surplus the local community was not allowed to consume, no taste for idle luxury, no jealous claim to private property, no exorbitant desire for power, no institutional war. Though scholars have long contemptuously dismissed the "myth of the Golden age," it is their scholarship, rather than the myth, that must now be questioned.

Such a society had indeed come into existence at the end of the last Ice Age, if not before, when the long process of domestication had come to a head in the establishment of small, stable communities with an abundant and varied food supply; communities whose capacity to produce a surplus of storable grain gave security and adequate nurture to the young. The rise and vitality was enhanced by vivid biological insight."[54]

Even George Gilder, the wealthy, archconservative Republican known for his denigrating remarks about women, admits that few men can attain psychological maturity without intimate association with a woman. She has, "as part of her very sexuality, a sense of the future: a sense of evolution and growth, a notion of deferring pleasures for future gains, a sense of the phases and seasons of life, a devotion to the value of the individual human being. These sentiments are the very source of human morality."[55]

The golden age of the matriarchy echoes in our mind as the lost Garden of Eden. It is our Paradise Lost. We have been unable to reenter the garden for the last ten thousand years. Instead, we have wandered around this beautiful earth, killing every life form with which we come in contact. We have now finally reached the point of destroying the earth itself. If we are to survive as a species, we must be able to balance the relationships between women and men and our different ways of seeing the world. Such a balance is vital for the survival of the species and for individual human beings to achieve our highest spiritual goal, mergence with the Divine Oneness. But this is stuff for a later discussion.

Let us now see how we got kicked out of the garden. In all fairness, let us say at this point that the blame cannot be placed solely on one gender or the other. While the men were responsible for the wars that reeked havoc on the agricultural civilizations of Egypt, Mesopotamia, the Indus Valley, among others, there was also a flaw in the women's social structure that gave rise to wide-scale male rebellion against the matriarchy. Thus, the loss of the Garden of Eden was an event brought on by the evolutionary immaturity of both genders, just as our return to it will require the advanced maturity of both genders.

## Brother Rule

Social cohesion under mother-rule was the kinship bond that brought groups together in mutual cooperation. The bond was maternal because early groups did not grasp paternal relationships due to the earliest taboos that placed sex outside the realm of one's community. Simply put, the connection between sexuality and childbearing was unknown to primitive people, as was the role of father.[56] The kinship group consisted of the mothers, their brothers, and the mothers' children. This kinship bond was the basis of the clan and clan confederation and both social formations were subject to the same taboos. You could not eat or kill anyone in the group, nor could you have sex with anyone in the group. While this created peace within the group, it created a different social stress—one that was keenly felt by the men. However, creation of the tribe solved the problem of sexual partners. The tribe consisted of two clan confederations in which members of one confederation could now have sex with the members of the other confederation. This was a big breakthrough for everyone.

During the entire Paleolithic Age women-rule prevailed. During this time, it was believed that only women held the divine power to give life. As child bearers and nurturers, women generally took charge of growing things to feed each other and the young. They became the producers, storers, and distributors of food, and they were the stewards of the land that they used for cultivation. They were the providers. Women assumed this position based upon the rituals and knowledge that they received as daughters of the Great Goddess.

Yet, despite the fullness of the matriarchal worldview and its vast accomplishments, it was based, after all, on false information. The mystery of life was not created out of blood; it was created from the egg of the female and the sperm of the male. When the men discovered that it was their sperm that created life—and not their blood—it greatly reinforced their sense of superiority and was an essential factor in bringing the value system of matriarchy to an end. It was now not women who gave birth, but men. The women were only the vessel to nurture the new life.

By this time in history, the surplus wealth generated by agriculture required that men take a greater role in its protection and distribution. The men had responsibility for educating the male teenagers in their clan and initiating them into manhood as conditions for assuming their role in society. They had also established strong bonds through the rituals of making men *blood brothers*.

This period of time in which men gained greater social power was called the *fratriarchy*, or period of brother-rule. Fratriarchy, the transition period between matriarchy and patriarchy, was a period of staggering social upheaval that paved the way for patriarchal rule and the systematic repression of women. The scars suffered by men and women during this period still stir in our cultural angst and rise from our subconscious, causing many of our nightmares even today.

Whereas the matriarchy corresponded largely to the Paleolithic Age, which extended from the earliest known use of stone tools to the end of the Pleistocene Epoch around ten thousand years ago, fratriarchy corresponded roughly to the Neolithic Period that dated roughly from fifteen thousand years to six thousand years ago.

Fratriarchy began with the expansion and authority of the mothers' brothers in tribal decision-making, particularly over the issue of property management. Property had begun to increase as stockbreeding and gardening replaced hunting and gathering. The advances in trading and specialized production also increased wealth. The authority of the men had also increased due to blood brotherhoods.

Still, it was the women who controlled the property, primarily because they invented it. In short, they invented the techniques to domesticate animals; they also invented the practices of gardening which, in turn, led to crop production and the agrarian revolution. Women also discovered the wealth of caves in fashioning commercial products out of the jewels, metals, and other precious stones.

The evidence for women's original control of wealth is universal. It can be traced through women's control of landed property. They controlled it because they were the first to farm it. As such, they named these parcels after the Goddess. In Europe; for example, as late as the Roman Empire, the landholding was still called a *latifundia*, meaning founded by the Goddess Lat. In Greece, a landholding was *temenos*, land belonging to the Moon. In Attica, the land unit was a *demos*, derived from Demeter (Mother Goddess).

Throughout Africa, the Middle East, and the Far East, the same situation prevailed.

Archaeologists believe that the earliest agricultural cultures were those of India, Mesopotamia, and Egypt. But logic dictates that there must also have been great agricultural civilizations in the heart of Africa where the oldest human civilizations took root. More research is required to learn this truth. In any case, agriculture flourished under the matriarchy. People were able to amass great wealth and create sophisticated cultures. In areas where the soil and climate prevented it, the populations remained nomadic. This created a split in the lifestyle of the human race. Those with benign climate and good soil developed agricultural civilizations. Those who lived in cold climates or lacked good soil remained nomadic.

In time, the nomadic tribes started to invade the agricultural civilizations and the ability of the people to protect themselves against these invaders became a pressing problem. The males had to mobilize for war in completely new ways. In fact, these circumstances created the activity of war, as we understand it today.

To understand the warrior's role in matriarchal society, we must go back to the idea of *blood revenge*. Blood revenge gave rise to the system of *regulated punishment* and *counter punishment* between two communities. It was an organized bloodletting. This system is still practiced by many primitive tribes today.

The origin of this practice was due to people's lack of understanding of the cause of death and other personal tragedies. They did not believe that death could occur naturally. Consequently, whoever died had to be killed by the influence of a stranger or enemy, either directly or indirectly, through magic. This made it imperative that the men band together to punish those who had brought harm to their kin.

Just as *blood kinship* was established on a communal basis, so also *blood revenge* was communal. As Evelyn Reed tells us, "The whole community was held responsible for the actions of each individual member. It was not necessary that any specific culprit be found and killed in reprisal for the death of a kinsman – any member of his community would suffice to satisfy the claims of blood."[57]

In its inception, blood revenge followed the mother-line. When a man died, his brothers and uncles were his avengers. When a woman died, her avengers were her sons, brothers, and maternal uncles.

Usually, when a clan member died, the elders set themselves the task to find out who the enemy was. This could entail some form of magical divination. Upon determining who caused the death, the kinsmen would set out to find and slay the culprit. Women were never held accountable for death and thus were never sought out and killed. It was the general belief that *death-giving* was the natural responsibility of men, just as life-giving was the natural responsibility of women.

Blood revenge, of course, would call forth retaliation from the other clan and a *hereditary feud* would become established. The situation destabilized early clan and tribal relations, causing hatred and bitterness between neighbors and keeping everyone in a state of ceaseless fear and trouble.

To alleviate this condition, the mothers and their brothers instituted the *principle of equivalence*.[58] In its advanced stage, this principle was enacted through two universal expressions, the *prearranged combat* and the *gift exchange* that followed it. Again as Reed explains, usually the two opposing sides met "periodically for the purpose of settling grievances between them which had accumulated over the preceding period. These combats are variously called the *regulated fight*, the *standup fight*, the *vengeance fight*, the *expiatory combat*, the *pitched battle*, and *cyclical warfare*. In some regions, these fights occurred on call; in others they were an annual event; and still others they occurred every five years or more."[59]

The fights were conducted according to specific rules, agreed upon by both sides, and supervised the authorities. As soon as the grievances were settled, they called a halt to the bloodshed and the warriors of both sides joined together after the battle to exchange gifts and restore peace.

Normally, no more than a few warriors on each side were killed. In time, the combat became more ritualized and abstract. Among some people, it even turned into a dance, the "dance of death."

The combat and gift exchange practices turned into funeral festivals that led to the Olympic contest of ancient Greece. These then evolved into the worldwide Olympic contest held today.

Not all adaptations, however, became so civilized. Among some tribes, self-mutilization replaced death. Sometimes a single individual served as a sacrifice to expiate the crimes of his people. In this tradition, we find the source of the idea of the *scapegoat*, which was originally human and later became an animal sacrifice with the onset of patriarchal society.

It should be obvious at this point that this kind of combat among tribal people is not the source of modern warfare as we understand it today where the purpose is to kill or maim as many people—as quickly as possible—in order to exterminate or control them, and, thereby, also control their land and property. Many anthropologists, beginning with Ashley Montagu, have demonstrated that peace and nonviolence are normative, rather than the exception, among primitive people. Matthew Melko, for example, identified fifty-two societies with periods of peace (without any warfare) lasting more than a century. Melko pointed out that the emphasis on organized warfare in history creates a false impression that peace is rare.[60]

How then did the universal practice of ritual combat breakdown and, in so doing, give rise to the warfare and imperialism that we experience today? The answer lies in the breakdown of the matriarchy and the rules that governed the behavior of men.

The decline of the matriarchy did not begin with an act of war on the part of the men against women. It began with the concept of "private ownership."

The first inroads that men made against the institutions of women's power were in the becoming *male-mothers, husbands, and husband-mothers.* Later they would become *male priestesses.* And later still, out of the tradition of the sacred king, men would become kings or warlords.

The role of *male-mother* was the first roll of power that men held in the clan structure. It signified the mother's brother's role in protecting his sister and her children. It was a role initially based on kinship and maternal bloodline. In time, as property developed and the role of the brother's authority increased, it also came to signify power over the wealth of the mother-family, including the children. This power over wealth did not yet constitute ownership over that wealth, which under matriarchy was always communal, but rather it consisted of decision-making authority over its utility.

## The Husband

In contra-distinction to the role of male-mother was the role of *husband.* This role was filled by the stranger, whom the sister chose as her lover or mate. From the very beginning of the family unit, the brother and the husband were at odds. So profoundly troublesome was this relationship that it ultimately caused the downfall of the matriarchy. In the downfall that occurred, during the period of fratriarchy, men were pitted against each other in a schizophrenic bloodbath the likes of which society had never, nor will ever, see again. Human bloodletting reached a feverish pitch and all human identity was lost in a cultural inversion of such enormous proportions that it overthrew all social and gender relations. This phenomenon set up a tidal wave in the social subconscious and was so profound that it still affects us today. It induced all male-dominated religions to keep women in an inferior position, at all costs. Relentless programming by these religions is why men see women as inferior and why they need to keep women in a socially inferior position regardless of the destruction that this mentality causes. The cultural inversion also caused the establishment of the *father-family, private property,* and *the state* upon which all secular forms of male rule are now derived.

How did such an upheaval occur? To know this, we need to understand the conflict that existed in the roles men played as *mother's brother* and *husband*. The role of the mother's brother as male-mother has been explained. To understand the role of husband, we must take a look at how the institution of marriage evolved.

We have observed previously that much of the danger in having sexual relations was alleviated with the institution of the tribe in which men from one confederation in the tribe could mate with women in the other confederation. In this relationship, men from one confederation were considered to be *cross-cousins* to men in the other confederation. Yet this did not completely dispense with tension or bloodshed. In fact, with the advent of agriculture and the breakdown of the tribe into clan villages, many gains made by men were wiped out. As R. F. Fortune explains in the *Sorcerers of Dobu*:

> "One marries into a village of enemies, witches and sorcerers, some of whom are known to have killed or to be the children of those known to have killed members of one's own village. The night divides the villages – apart from lovemaking, 100 yards is as far as 1,000 or 10,000 for all practical purposes. Even roaming for lovemaking should be done while the night is still young. In the dark spaces between the villages the agents of death roam – the death-dealing spirits of the women and men of all other villages, witches and sorcerers all...."

The boys who go out for lovemaking then, go out with great boldness into a night filled with terrors. They are usually supported by a good conscience in that they have not given offense to the adults of other villages, a fact not so true of their parents. Nevertheless, they go into dangerous territory, for it is well known that in matters of sorcery and witchcraft, native vengeance may visit the sins of the fathers, mothers, and mother's brothers upon the children down the generations."[61]

This sheds light on the conditions that preceded the institution of marriage. *Pair-union* evolved slowly in human history because of the dangers involved. In fact, it did not emerge until fifteen thousand to eight thousand years ago, tens of thousands of years after human society began.

Therefore, the right of safe passage made possible by the institution of cross-cousins, did not necessarily alleviate the suspicions and fears between the men of the two moieties, or between men of different villages.

In the earliest stage of *matrimony*, which means *mother-marriage*, or, more precisely, *marriage by mother-in-law*, the husband was little more than a visitor to his wife's community. He did not start out owning his own house with his wife. Rather, he was given accommodations in the male clubhouse reserved for strangers and visiting husbands. There, under the surveillance of his wife's kin, as well as the suspicions of other strangers, he slept and took his meals.[62] Under such circumstances, he had to enter by night the dwelling of the mother of the woman with whom he wanted to have sexual relations. In most cases, he had to sneak in and out of the hut under threat of physical harm. The Japanese still have a word for marriage, *home-iri*, which means "to slip by night into the house."[63] Many primitive people today are still subject to this ritual of sexual intercourse. In time, in order to relieve the situation, the mothers would act as the go-between to bring the lovers together out of harm's way. As Evelyn Reed claims, "the fearsome old witch gradually became transformed into a proper mother-in-law, although she still remained a formidable figure, to be treated with great circumspection.[64]

As the ritual of *gift exchange* became more advanced, the mother's brother took on the role of go-between. This made the institution of marriage as much an expression of fraternal relations as it was of matrimony. Nonetheless, the transfer of the role of go-between from the mother to the brother did little to ease social tensions. In fact, it only aggravated them.

But let us not get ahead of ourselves. Marriage by mother-in-law was the original form of marriage, and the first form of family was the mother-family, not the father-family as exists today. As such, marriage in the early days occurred something like this. If a young woman wanted to have more than a surreptitious sexual relationship with a young man, she would propose marriage to him. In a preliterate society, she would invite the man to stay the night with her in her mother's house. In a literate society, like Egypt, she would send her lover a love poem. The idea was to have the girl's mother except him as her official son-in-law.

On such an occasion, the night would begin with the young man slipping into the house. Normally, he would leave before dawn, but now he would feign oversleep. The mother would rise before the young couple and upon seeing them, would go out and sit in front of the door, blocking the exit with her body.[65]

This meant that the matrimonial application had been accepted. Now the villagers, seeing the mother-in-law sitting before her dwelling, would gather to see what young man would emerge. Neighboring villages would be notified and everyone would gather. They would circle around the old woman and stare. Into this glare of curiosity seekers, the young couple would emerge and sit beside the mother. The spectators would remain for a time staring in silence. The staring ceremony made the engagement official.[66]

Such an event made the man a *husband* (i.e., one who was *bound to the house*). He would now assume certain responsibilities, like the hard work of crop and animal *husbandry*. In agricultural villages; for example, after all the other villagers had dispersed, the mother-in-law would turn to the young man, put a digging stick in his hand, and say, "Go, make a garden."

Marriage and the mother-family began simultaneously with farming. With the advance to an agricultural economy, tribal society reached its peak. Thereafter, it began to decay. The interlocking system of clans began to break up into separate clans, each forming a separate village community. Matrimonial arrangements then began to be made on a clan-to-clan basis and, ultimately, a family-to-family basis. Yet the mother-family was not to last for long because of the unresolved schizophrenia it created in the men. Men became split down the middle in their roles as husband and brother. They were forced to lead two lives in two separate villages. Such pressure affected not only the husbands and brothers, as individuals, but also the relations of brother and sister and husband and wife. It also created turmoil between intermarrying families and their clans.

The crux of the problem was that when a man left his own community for his wife's community, he became subject to divided interests and loyalties. His basic rights, responsibilities, and allegiances were with his sisters and other kin. This inhibited the fuller development of his relation with his wife and children. On the other hand, the wife was not subject to these pressures directly. As a resident of her own community, she was surrounded and supported by her mother's kin. She had no responsibility of any kind to her husband's kin.

The men were put in a no-win situation, which ultimately dragged everyone down. The conflict between brother and husband existed not only in the relationship between the men of different clans but also existed in the mind of each man as he was forced to play both roles. In his own community, he was a brother in the house of his mother and sisters. He remained their economic and social companion no matter how many husbands came and went. As a brother, he was a male pillar in his own matrilineal community. As head of his sister's lineage and household, he held authority as the chief disciplinarian and protector and he was honored and obeyed. He also had authority for transmitting the ritual heritage of the clan. When he grew too old to carry on his role, he selected the most capable nephew and trained him in the duties of any ceremonial positions which he held. Yet, even though he had respect, authority, and responsibility for overseeing the family's wealth and the clan's well being, he had no house of his own. The house belonged to his mother and the other women in the family. Thus, he had no property to which he could bring his wife and raise a family and, therefore, had to go to his wife's village if he wanted to be with her.

This dependency put the man in a very untenable situation. In his wife's village, a man had few rights as a husband and none as a father to his wife's children, since they were cared for by their mother and their uncle. The man also suffered the humiliation of being under the thumb of his wife's kinsmen.

Anthropologists, like Reed, have found that among matriarchal remnants, "a wife's brother may make almost any demands on the sister's husband and these must be fulfilled. Failure to meet the demands of a wife's brother are grounds for terminating the marriage, and the brother will tell his sister to request the husband to leave."[67]

Hostility between brother and husband was also aggravated by the ancient ignorance of the cause of natural death and accidental injury. Fear and suspicion governed their relationship so that each believed the other was attempting to destroy him through foul magic.

As the value of a clan's wealth increased, the antagonism between the wife's brother and husband increased, and so did the antagonism between sister and brother and between husband and wife.

As the tribe broke down into agricultural villages, the safety of cross cousin relations also broke down and heterogeneous men were thrown together in village life. Suspicion and threats increased. Also, with the decay of the tribe, fewer men were available to support the village women. In some cases, an individual brother was required to provide for an individual sister and also contribute to the support of his wife's family.

In actuality, the big problem was that no matter how hard a man might try to become integrated into his wife's community, there were regular upheavals in his marriage and a permanent dissolution of it at death. An attempted solution to the problem consisted in the husband and wife spending time alternately in each other's village. This did not help much. It only made the wife subject to the same abuse as her husband in her village. Often, she would leave and go back to her village, taking the children with her. No matter how dear the feelings were between the husband and the children, fatherhood still had no meaning.

## Fatherhood

Fatherhood had its humble beginnings in the role of *husband-mother*. It did not originate in the human mind as a biological fact, but rather as a social relationship between a woman's husband and her children. It began as the usurpation of the brother's role of assisting in the care and protection of a woman's children, and, perhaps more to the point, in the husband's usurpation of ownership of the wife, her children, and property. Among the Aryans, who are the oldest known patriarchal tribe, the word for father simply meant *owner*. Among Semitic tribes, the word for father, (*ab* or *abu*) also meant owner.[68]

The husband's right to fatherhood was socially established in a ritual called the *couvade*. The central feature of this ritual was the man imitating the women after childbirth.

> "As couvade is usually described, the wife, directly after giving birth, goes about her daily activities without further ado. But the husband takes to his hammock or bed, "lying in" for a time. He is treated as an invalid and subjected to strict taboos and rules of avoidance. He is expressly forbidden to do work of any kind, must not engage in violent activities such as hunting, and may not touch any weapons. He is especially forbidden to eat flesh foods. He undergoes a period of complete fasting from which he is gradually

released by being fed weak gruel or mash, normally given to infants. Old women minister to his needs, supervise his observance of the taboos, and assist his recovery."[69]

Originally, couvade allowed the man to nurture only his wife's male children. In this act, two males from different communities were joined together as *father* and *son* or, more precisely, *husband-mother* and son.

By practicing the couvade, a man was giving a public demonstration that he was not killing anything—animal, vegetable, or human. He was, therefore, not liable to blood reprisal if any unforeseen accident or death should occur.

Even so, the couvade did not make the man a full-fledged father, as we understand the term today. The people were still ignorant of the biological connection between father and child. And socially, there were still significant limitations put on the relationship between a husband-mother and the children of his wife. For example, the man was obliged by matriarchal law to teach his sister's children his magical knowledge, which was the means whereby he was able to protect his kin from outsiders and determine enemy intentions. He could not, under any circumstances, share this information with his wife's children. This would constitute subversion.

Thus, we see that the mother-family was at constant and profound odds with the rules of the matriarchal system as a whole. This contradiction was never resolved within the system.

The schism in men's roles continued to fester, fueled by fear, ignorance, and the ancient heritage of *blood revenge*. The conflict between brother and husband increased as they began to see each other as the primary cause of each other's problems.

In order for the father-family to evolve, the role of the woman's brother as the guardian and protector of his sister's children had to end. This meant that the blood kinship bond, which had existed in the human mind since time immemorial, had also to be dissolved. Such a changed required a social upheaval of impossible magnitude. And yet, such an upheaval had to occur in order for the husband-mother to become the husband- father and to own or beget (to *get* from the wife and her brother) a child as his *own* and to create the father-family as a social unit.

As Evelyn Reed says, "It was not enough for the father to beget his own son by "getting" it from his wife. Only when the mother's brother relinquished all claims to his sister's son could the father acquire it as his *own* or *own begotten* or *only begotten son*. This, in turn, required that the mother's brother abandon his sister and sister's children and *cleave* to his wife and wife's children."[70]

Because a man could not belong to two clans at the same time, for him to enter a primary relationship with his wife meant giving up his blood bond to his mother and brothers. This was a betrayal of the greatest order. It meant that for the first time in human history, matrilineal kin would be in opposition to one another.[71] It meant the breakdown of social consciousness as a primary force and set the conditions for the development of individual consciousness as a primary force in history. In order to achieve this transition it meant abandoning the idea of kinship and replacing it with the idea of people as property. It was a horrific transition made necessary by the need to move beyond an evolutionary dead end in human social formations.

Murder and treachery now came between men of the maternal brotherhood, who from the beginning of human society had regarded each other's lives as sacred and inviolable. The ancient idea of an absolute blood bond broke down. As tribal feeling decayed and family feeling increased, fratricide spread across the earth. Brothers killed brothers; uncles killed nephews; and nephews killed uncles. This reality is born out in archetypal myths. According to the story of Cain and Abel, fratricide was the first type of murder to be committed. In the mythology of ancient Rome, the city is founded as the result of a fratricide, when the twins Romulus and Remus quarreled over who had the favor of the gods. Romulus became Rome's first king and namesake after killing his brother.

In the Hindu epic *Mahābhārata*, Arjuna killed Karna, whom he did not know was his brother.[72]

In studying the history and myths of this period, leading anthropologist Bronislaw Malinowski reports, "Thus in real life as well as in myth we see that the situation… is at cross variance with tribal law and conventional tribal ideals. According to law and morals, two clan brothers or a maternal uncle and his nephews are friends and allies and have all feelings and interest in common. In real life to a certain degree and quite openly in myth, they are enemies who cheat each other and murder each other. Suspicion and hostility have replaced brotherly love and union." [73]

Most primitive tribes today retain tales of brothers who kill each other simultaneously and of the maternal uncle who sacrifices his sister's son.[74]

Perhaps the most terrible feature of this difficult transition in human relations was the practice of killing the firstborn son. This act, known variously to anthropologists as *blood redemption*, the *sacrifice*, or *redemptive sacrifice*, was a ritual offering to the mother's brother or more often the *ghost* of the mother's brother on the part of the father to allow the transfer of ownership of the family to himself, while appeasing the established order of matrilineal relations.

In his book, *Folkways*, William Graham Sumner says, [C]hild sacrifice expresses the deepest horror and suffering produced by experience of the human lot. Men must do it. Their interests demand it, however much it might pain them. Human sacrifices may be said to have been universal. They lasted down to the half-civilized stage of all nations and sporadically even later, and they have barely ceased among the present half civilized peoples. They are not primarily religious. They are a reaction of men under the experience of the ills of life.[75]

In the transition from matriarchy to patriarchy, two opposing rights came into collision and produced the highest form of tragedy. The right of the mother's brother and the right of the father were irreconcilable. The mother's brother could not relinquish his inherited *blood bond* to his sister, her children, and the clan. Neither could the father share his inherited obligation for *blood revenge*. In an attempt to solve this awful dilemma and stay the disintegration of human society at every level, human beings were forced to offer their first born as the highest *blood gift*.

## Partitioning the Firstborn

Apparently, there was no other way to sever the bond of the matrilineal bloodline that created the divided *two-father family*. The very form of the sacrifice is symbolic; it is sometimes called *the partitioning* of the child. Anthropologists and archaeologists have found evidence of child sacrifice in Assyrian and Canaanite religions. Phoenicians, Carthaginians, and other members of early states sacrificed infants to their gods.[76]

In the early days, the Israelites also sacrificed their firstborn sons. In Micah 6:7, the prophet asks God if he still wants a sacrifice of the firstborn son as a sacrifice for his sin. However, by the time the Jewish patriarchs had emerged, well after the coming and going of many Middle East empires, their Father God no longer demanded human sacrifice. We are told that God was willing to accept an animal sacrifice as an act of blood redemption in place of Abraham's firstborn son. In the Passover legends, the sacrifice of a lamb became the price of redemption.

Certainly, the importance of the sacrifice of the firstborn son still echoes in Jewish history. An example is the saga of the ten plagues God inflicted upon the Egyptians, the last of which he struck down their firstborn sons (Exodus 11:5, 12:12). This act served as the requirement that the male firstborn of man and beast in Israel were to be devoted to God.[77] In Numbers 3:13, it says, "Because all the firstborn are mine; for on the day that I smote all the firstborn in the land of Egypt I hallowed unto me all the firstborn in Israel, both man and beast: mine shall they be: I am the Lord."

In this case, we have a people who had already passed through a terrible time of child killing. But in the beginning, because every man was at once mother's brother to his sister's son and a father to his wife's son, all men were stained with the blood of the slain firstborn sons. Whether the child was the son of a sister or the son of a wife, he was the victim who was partitioned. Finally, since a woman was both the sister of a brother and the wife of a husband, every mother also suffered the agony of the sacrifice of her firstborn son. All humanity paid the price for adherence to an outworn kinship system.

Through the idea of blood redemption the same human psychology that originated totemism and human sacrifices to the goddess, now created a new form of blood sacrifice. This ritual was essentially an act to resolve a property dispute. Yet, once begun, it was difficult to stop. Given the social upheaval, the brother's ghost took on an ever more fearsome and insatiable supernatural form. The brother's ghost became the Guardian Ghost, a reactionary creation who, in time, became ever hungrier for blood. Where formerly only firstborn sons were offered, in time more and more children were sent as offerings to appease the new gods. Evelyn Reed offers the following observation: "how could men gauge the demands of these unseen Baals and Molochs who, after being propitiated with sacrificial offerings, continued to imperil them with famines, wars and other calamities? They could only pour out more and more sacrifices to these voracious demons—while the demons could never open a human mouth to cry 'Enough!'"[78]

As the social upheaval continued, the *magic* of the women, the Great Goddess, and, in fact, the entire meaning of life began to lose its hold over the minds of human beings. Men now began to demand access to the magical formulas of the women. The process for the transference of knowledge and power began with the men dressing themselves as women so as to appear as women to the Goddess. In some societies, the *male-priestesses* were ritually castrated in order to become women. In time, they began to speak as oracles, and in so doing take took control over the social consciousness.

As the bloodshed between men increased, the traditional role of sacred king also began to change. Normally, the strongest, most virile male filled this role, which entailed living with the Queen for a period of time and then being ritually slaughtered as an act of blood redemption for the people. This role was central to the well-being of the people, and therefore it became a natural point of origin for male political power. In time, however, the sacred king became the *king*, a supreme male authority—as we understand the term today. The early King still remained the mate of the Queen, but he was no longer sacrificed. Instead, a substitute was chosen to be sacrificed.

Usurpation of the queen's power by the king required that he knew what the queen knew. In short, he had to steal the secrets of the Goddess. Consequently, all early tales of the first kings ascending to power contained explanations of how the King stole the secrets of the Goddess and therein achieved immortality and divinity. Before this came to pass, however, there would be more bloodshed. Toward the end of the fratriarchy, the war gods emerged. These were the most bloodthirsty gods of all. Now the sacrifices of king surrogates and firstborn males no longer sufficed. Mass child sacrifices became a custom. If a man had no child of his own to offer, he had to buy, steal, or borrow one. Such mass sacrifices were observed and recorded among the Carthaginians and Canaanites in the Middle East and among the Aztecs and Incas of the Americas.

What great force was finally able to eliminate the ritual of blood redemption and bring an end to the tide of blood? It was the origin of the idea of private property, which accomplished this deed as nothing else could.[79]

As Evelyn Reed explains, "the driving necessity to achieve the one father-family and do away with the divided mother-family opened the road to private property. Private property, in turn, became the indispensable means for severing all chains to the old social order and inaugurating the new patriarchal, class-based society. The state, which arose later, consolidated and legalized both private property and the father family with its line of descent, inheritance, and succession from fathers to sons."[80]

Out of the agonizing process of the decaying matriarchy, with its tribal politics and values and rituals of the magical worldview, emerged the new social formation of patriarchy, with its father-family, private property, class-based society, and the new male-based worldview of religion.

Let us now look at how this new world order came about.

# The Rise of Patriarchy

THE CHANGE FROM BROTHER-RULE to father-rule created an entirely new system of human organization. Patriarchy literally means father-rule. This system, which began ten thousand years ago, is still firmly established today. Much of what we believe about ourselves as human beings derives from ten thousand years of social conditioning under the institutions of father-rule.

Today, whether we live in the Far East, the Middle East, Africa, Europe, the Americas, or the islands of the world, we are subject to the values and institutions of patriarchy. Regardless of our race, nationality, religion, or any other collective identity, we are subject to the same interpretation of gender relations. Just as females were once the authority figures governing human society, now males have that role.

In the development of the human species, despite our long history of accumulated knowledge and wealth, the instinctive (genetic) use of brute force was applied to the accumulation of even more power, more knowledge, and more wealth. It is a human characteristic to always strive for more. Our thirst is unquenchable. This drive is in the nature of our evolutionary pattern.

To dominate the female of the species has been an ancient primordial urge in the male. Once this was achieved in a social organization, this drive provided the basis for extending male rule across the planet.

The onset of patriarchy was established when marriage became a form of ownership. Women were reduced to the status of property in an arrangement aimed at resolving the conflict of the sister's brother or uncle with the husband. The consequence of this mentality gave rise to patriarchal rule, which came to include the enslavement of conquered peoples, the creation of the militarized city-state, the creation of class society, and the justification for male action in the pursuit of wealth and power regardless of consequence. Patriarchy also created patriarchal religions that hold women responsible for the fall of man from God's grace and for eternally threatening his sexual purity. For these reasons, women deserved every punishment and humiliation that man could bestow on them. To understand the programming of modern men and women, we need to understand how this male onslaught occurred.

## The Bride Price

Under matriarchy, we saw how marriage was arranged by the wife's mother, who acted as go-between to bring the lovers together and sanctioned the marriage by accepting the man as her official son-in-law. After a time, however, the mother's brother assumed the role of go-between. Such brother-sanctioned marriages were part of the tradition of blood revenge and gift exchange that characterize the relationship of men during the matriarchy. In the case of marriage, the mother's brother offered his niece in marriage to a husband for the ostensible purpose of achieving peaceful relations. In return, the husband would offer gifts of his own.

Such exchange of gifts became more significant as the accumulation of private wealth was made possible by the improved economy of agriculture and stockbreeding. In addition, the abundance of food led to greater populations and to the requirement for greater management skills needed to create wealth and to divide the labor.

As the desire to accumulate more wealth was engendered in the minds of men, the system of gift exchange, now under the control of the men, underwent a critical transformation. As the family's and the clan's wealth came gradually under the control of brother-rule, the brother also came to control his sister's or his niece's children, who were the indispensable vehicles for protecting family property in one's old age, as well as from one generation to the next.

How then did the husband come to supplant the wife's brother's or uncle's control of the family unit and inherit its wealth? The turning point came when the *marriage gift*, offered by the husband, changed into a *bride price*. At this point in human history, the *gift exchange* between men changed into a different kind of transaction—the exchange of personal property.

Robert Briffault, in his classic work *The Mothers*, explains the transition from marriage gift to the bride price:

> "The purchasable wife was impossible in the most primitive cultural stages, not only because the men have no notion of any commercial exchange, but because they possess no fundable property, and are therefore destitute of purchasing power....Only at a very definite stage of cultural evolution has the man become an owner of transferable and fundable property, and in a position to drive the market, and to commute all contributions to the woman's family by a lump payment. That position was attained only when he became an owner of domesticated cattle, his first form of real property. Marriage by purchase in the proper sense is accordingly not found at all in Australia, Melanesia, Polynesia, or in America, where no domesticated cattle, and consequently no man owned wealth, existed. It is in pastoral societies, or in societies that have passed through pastoral stages, in Africa, Asia, and Europe, that the purchase power of the bride-gift developed.[81]

Evelyn Reed adds, "The importance of cattle in the development of private property has long been recognized. Cattle were very valuable in the early period of farming; they served as draft and pack animals, and they provided food for the larder and byproducts for craft industries. In addition, livestock reproduced themselves, multiplying all these benefits. These were the reasons cattle became the earliest form of movable property to be bartered for wives.[82]

Anthropologists refer to this primitive exchange of cattle for a wife as *cattle marriage*. Cattle marriages fall into both categories—gift-exchange and bride price—and it is often difficult for anthropologists to determine the difference when they analyze the behavior of existing primitive tribes. Yet upon close inspection, a distinction can be made. For those tribes who had not passed into the bride-price marriage, the recipient group or family did not permanently retain the cattle as their property. Instead, the animals were kept in constant circulation, and offered out again when another young man or woman in the group sought marriage. In this situation, there was no purchase transaction, simply a gift exchange between groups. In this gift-exchange marriage, the maternal uncle, as the older male in the mother family, received the cattle offered by the husband in exchange for his needs. But he was not an independent individual who could take possession of the cattle as his personal property. He was only the custodian of the cattle, acting in the interest of the group. In other words, *brother right* was still dependent upon *mother right* and property still followed the mother's line (matrilineal).

The situation, however, was wholly different for the husband who was attempting to become the sole father in an undivided family. Evelyn Reed explains it this way:

> [T]he husband's opportunity came from the fact that the cattle exchange for his wife gave him claims to her children as his own. Even if the marriage broke up, these claims remained valid and could only be voided through the return of the cattle. This was not always possible if, for example, the cattle had been passed on to secure a wife for the brother of the bride or another person in the clan.

Cattle that died created further problems in the matter of refunds. It is not difficult to see how the passing of cattle as marriage gifts would falter in the face of claims and counter-claims regarding the possession of children or the refund of cattle. Subtly, but inextricably, cattle marriage passed over from an interchange relationship to an exchange relationship involving ownership of property. With the advent of the bride price and child price, the road was paved for the private ownership of cattle in the hands of the husband and father who, as an individual, could dispose of them as he wished.[83]

Through such a transition, the role of husband and husband-mother became *father* (i.e., the owner). Therefore, we can also see that fatherhood did not originate with the human understanding of the fathers biological role in childbirth, but with property rights. Anthropologists have long observed that the claims by the father on the woman's children was of equal, if not greater, importance than his claim on the woman. A son meant family strength, a helping hand, and an heir to accumulated private property. A daughter meant an exchange value of more cattle.

In ancient Mesopotamia, laws regarding bride price appear in the Code of Hammurabi. It is not the payment of the bride price that is prescribed, but the regulation of its various aspects. For example:

A man who paid the bride price but looked for another bride would not get a refund, but he would if the father of the bride refused the match.

If a wife died without sons, her father was entitled to the return of her dowry, minus the value of the bride price.

The practice of the bride price is referred to in the Old Testament, (Exodus 22:16–17) where it says: "

> If a man seduces a virgin who is not pledged to be married and sleeps with her, he must pay the bride price, and she

shall be his wife. If her father absolutely refuses to give her to him, he must still pay the bride price for virgins."

In Deuteronomy 22:28-29, it similarly states: "

> If a man happens to meet a virgin who is not pledged to be married and rapes her and they are discovered, he shall pay the girl's father fifty shekels of silver. He must marry the girl, for he has violated her. He can never divorce her as long as he lives."

Even today, marriage by bride price is still the norm in many countries. In the Philippines, India, Thailand, China, Afghanistan, and many countries in the Middle East, Central Asia, Africa, as well as the Solomon Islands and Papua New Guinea, bride price is still practiced as a way for men to buy women and thus make them their property. The price will vary according to different factors. In India today, the price of a bride can be as little as four thousand to thirty thousand Indian rupees, the equivalent of eighty-eight to six hundred and sixty US dollars.[84]

Even in the United States today, some women are subjected to *forced marriages* and some children are still subject to *child marriages*. These victims receive no help from the US government or any of its agencies.[85] The State of New York; for example, did not make child marriages illegal until 2017. In many states, it still remains permissible.

*Child price* was a concomitant development of bride price whereby the children also became the property of the father to do with as he desired. In the beginning, this practice was a progressive development in that it ended the ritual slaughter of children, which was the terrible consequence of brother/husband conflict.

## The Father-Family

With the advent of bride price, however, women lost control over whom they wanted to marry. Now men made the deals and the marriage contracts. In time, these deals were no longer made between mother's brothers; they were made between the husbands and fathers of different families. By degrees, the women came more under control of their husbands. "Through cattle payments, the husband became the father and took possession of his wife. The women's brother now had to relinquish all claims to his sister's children. Once the brothers and mother's brothers were eliminated, the husbands and fathers could consolidate their supremacy over their wives and children as their *own* family."[86] Nonetheless, for unmarried women, when a father is not present, we still find occurrences where a woman's brother controls her life and forces her into a marriage in return for money for himself. Since then, marriage has been one of property relations. In this manner, women not only became dominated by men, but also enslaved by them. Women were the first slaves of patriarchal society and have remained so, in one respect or another, for the last ten thousand years.

The fact that the *father-family* originated as a *property contract*—and was not based upon knowledge of biology—accounts for the variation of patriarchal marriages observed by anthropologists. Variations include *leviratic marriage, ghost marriage*, and *woman-to-woman marriage*.[87]

Leviratic marriage, which means husband's brother marriage, is the best known. If a husband dies before his wife bore him a son, one of his brothers would marry the widow and beget a son for him. This form of marriage was known throughout Europe, Africa, the Middle East, and Asia, and still exists today among tribal people.

Living with a woman was not relevant, she could live with whomever, but the children she bore went to the father's line of the deceased husband by virtue of the cattle payment that had been made for them.

Ghost marriage is a variation of the leviratic marriage, but, in this case, there is no need for the brother to marry his dead brother's widow. Instead, he can beget a son from any woman and credit the son to his dead brother's line. Even unmarried men, if they died without a son, could attain one after death by such means.

Finally, in the woman-to-woman marriage, a kinswoman of the deceased man contracts with another female to provide her with an heir. In doing so, the kinswoman becomes essentially a *female-husband*. There are also reported cases of *female-fathers*. As E. Adamson Hoebel tells us in *Man In The Primitive World*, "a married woman may pay the bride-price to obtain a second wife for the husband as a means of providing him with children. These children called their sire's first wife *father*, because she, after all, is the one who paid for them."[88]

These, then, are some of the arrangements made in the development of the father-family as it was based upon private property. In time, as laws came to support these marital arrangements, severe punishments awaited any man who tampered with these property rights, and in the case of unfaithfulness, which meant *theft*, the wife too could be severely punished.

Thus, women came to lose all the power that they enjoyed under matriarchal arrangements. As Evelyn Reed says, "With the consolidation of private property and the father-family, not only the matriarchy but the fratriarchy fell into ruins. The mother's brothers, abandoning their sisters, became the fathers of their own families and the owners of their own property. This left women with no male allies; they were completely at the mercy of the new social forces unleashed by property-based patriarchal society." [89]

Women and children, through monogamous marriage, became the first slaves owned by the husband. By the time the Aryans, entered India, their rules of marriage had already become one of complete domination and ownership. According to Aryan codes:

"In her childhood a girl should be under the will of her father; in her youth under that of her husband; her husband being dead, under the will of her sons. A woman should never enjoy her own will. Though of bad conduct or debauched, a husband must always be worshipped like a god by a good wife."[90]

The belief that women are no more than property, which has existed for the last ten thousand years, is responsible for the fall of humanity from grace —and not the fact that Eve offered to Adam the gift of knowledge in the Garden of Eden.

What sociologists call the *father-family* still remains, for most of the world, a glib euphemism for a self-serving male and his subordinate dependents, if not outright slaves. This remains the truth today despite the recent development of more equitable relationships within a few civilized nations. Marriage has always consisted of the relationship of owner and owned. Among more brutal men, this relationship becomes one of master and slave. The enslavement of women and children through marriage provided the precedent for many other people who were bought or sold under patriarchal rule.

Eventually, in place of the bride price, the *dowry* arrived on the human scene. The dowry was an economic inducement made by the father of the bride in order to get a man to marry his daughter. This began with the Aryans and was transmitted through India, Greek, and Roman cultures and still exists today in India among descendents of the Aryans. The ritual by which the father of the bride pays for the wedding ceremony and dinner is a version of the dowry that still exists today in most countries.

## Classification of Married Women

According to Shrii P. R. Sarkar, the classification of married women in Aryan-dominated India testifies to a long history of manipulation of women by men. About 7,000 seven thousand years ago, opportunistic men began dividing the social status of women into various categories, which included:

*Patnii*: a patnii enjoyed equal religious and social rights as her husband. Her children were entitled to all religious and social rights as their inheritance.

*Jáyá*: a jáyá was deprived of the religious rights, but was entitled to the social rights of her husband. Her children were entitled to the religious and social rights of their father.

*Bháryá*: A bháryá was not allowed any of the religious or social rights of her husband. But as the marriage was recognized, her children were entitled to the religious and social rights of their father. A bháryá was married only to perpetuate the lineage, not to give the woman dignity. That's why it was declared: Puttrárthe kriyate bháryá ("A bháryá is taken on only for the sake of male children").

*Kalatra*: Some time before the Buddhist age, the system of kalatra was introduced, but it did not receive encouragement in the Buddhist period. It remained in an obscure form, but later gained ascendancy in the post-Buddhist age. In this husband-wife relationship, the wife did not enjoy the religious and social rights of her husband. The children were also denied any of the paternal religious or social rights; they inherited their mother's gotra (clan village, or literally, hill), caste, and social rights. For instance, if the father was a Brahmin, an "intellectual", and the mother a Shúdra, their child did not receive its father's caste; it was put into the caste of its mother (i.e., the child was treated as a Shúdra). Needless to say, as the children of kalatras were not entitled to paternal religious and social rights, they were not permitted to keep fire either.[91] If a kalatra marriage was socially recognized, the children were entitled to the maternal religious and social rights. Only if their mother was permitted to keep fire did her children inherit the right to keep fire.

*Pratiloma*: In the cases where the father was of an upper caste and the mother was of a lower caste, offspring born under such an *anuloma* system (where a boy from an upper class can marry a girl from a lower class) were entitled to their father's gotra and caste, but not his religious and social rights. (This was the case in the patriarchal social system. But in the matrilineal social system the children would inherit the mother's gotra, caste, and social and religious rights.) Hundreds of castes and sub-castes were created due to the children born out of this pratiloma system.

You can easily understand from these various marriage systems that women were merely playthings in the hands of opportunistic, capricious men. Today their position has changed on paper, but the actual position remains virtually the same as before. People guided by righteous intellect should be vocal against these ugly customs and injustices to women. Further, they should work to abolish these things without any more delay. [92]

The transition from mother-rule to brother-rule to father-rule occurred unevenly in human history. Some primitive tribes still reflect the matriarchy, while a few uphold the fratriarchy. Most people of the world, however, are subject to patriarchal values and institutions. In India, for example, with the arrival of the Aryans, the matriarchy and the matrilineal system were thrown into chaos. It took thousands of years for society to stabilize. And today, the matriarchal order still prevails among the Khasias[93] and certain other primitive tribes due to the late arrival and insignificant influence of the patriarchal Aryans. Traces of matriarchy may still be found among the Malayalese, who live in remote areas south of India. On the other hand, despite being fundamentally Austrico-Dravidian, the Bengalis have, for the most part, accepted patriarchy because of their close contact with the Aryans. However, their social system remains a blending of the patrilineal and matrilineal systems. While their social life is still patriarchal on the surface, Bengalis still give predominance to the mother—not to father.[94]

By looking at the Aryan tribes, the earliest known patriarchal tribes, we can see how these changes from matriarchy to patriarchy came about.

# Aryans – the First Patriarchs

THE ARYANS WERE A nomadic people who originated in the Caucasus Mountains in southern Russia. Their primary means of subsistence was hunting. When it became too difficult to hunt, they started rearing cattle. The cattle became a transferable value and could be exchanged for women and other goods. Therefore, cattle eventually became the first form of money. The Aryans were Caucasian in race; their skin was white due to their northern environment.

According to Shrii P. R. Sarkar, "The merciless nature of Central Asia made their lives unbearable. Snowstorms diminished the numbers both of their people and of their animals, and there was a chronic shortage of animal fodder. Just to survive, they had to spend almost all their time collecting food. Not only did this acute food shortage force them to make unending efforts as a group to collect food and rear cattle, it also led to perpetual inter-group skirmishes and even slaughter."[95]

In these battles, those who were defeated were captured as slaves and the women were taken to the harems of the victors. The victorious clan would then occupy the hill (gotra) of the vanquished clan. The women were forcibly carried away, their hands bound in iron chains. Even to this day, some women in India wear iron bangles on their wrists after marriage—the symbol of their ancient slavery. Also during the marriage ceremony, in certain parts of India, the bride's clothes are tied to the clothes of the bridegroom. The enslavement of the defeated gotra was a great humiliation, especially for the women. Sometimes during the battle, the men would strike the heads of the women with an axe, causing blood to flow. Today, at the time of marriage, women put a red dot on their foreheads, which is a symbol of this ancient bloodletting.[96]

In this warrior-dominated culture, in which there was constant fighting, a class of intellectuals emerged who were called the r'sis. The warriors bowed their heads to these benefactors and began to follow their ideas. Their ideology became known as "Arsa Dharma" (Religion of the Sages).

Somewhere between fifteen thousand and ten thousand years ago, at the dawn of Aryan patriarchy, the Aryans were still living in the steppes of the Caucasian mountains. They had no written script so they had to memorize the words of the rśis. Their teachings became known as shruti (literally "ear").

## The Start of Patriarchal Religion

At this time, the average intelligence of the Aryan people was very low and most were unable to understand the discourses of the intellectuals. They simple called their teaching "veda" which means "knowledge".[97] As was common at the time, the people believed that their rśis (priests) were superior beings and their wisdom came directly from the mouths of the gods. The r'sis could hear the words of god in their minds. Thus, like in every religion, the r'sis told the people that their words came directly from their god's lips and were therefore infallible. The r'sis sang hymns to their nature gods, performed rituals, gave eulogies, and offered plant and animal sacrifices. The average Aryan knew nothing about mysticism or spiritual practices.

According to Shrii P.R. Sarkar, "In that age of undeveloped science, they thought that smoke and the clouds in the sky were the same thing. That was why they burned ghee in sacrificial fires: they wanted to make smoke out of it to propitiate the different gods. They believed that the smoke would soar into the sky and turn into clouds; that rain would pour down from the clouds and nourish the earth causing an abundance of trees, plants and grass to sprout forth; and that their domestic animals, strengthened by the fresh grass, would multiply. That was why animal sacrifices were very common among the different groups and tribes."[98]

The deities of the Aryans demonstrated no spiritual power. Rather, they were a typical pantheon of gods (devas) who represented the forces of nature. The sky-god was called *Dyaus Pitar*. He was considered the father of the gods. His name, following the Aryan expansion into the west, became *Zu* in Babylonia, *Zeus Pater* in Athens, and *Ju Piter* (Jupiter) in Rome. He fathered Surya (sun), Agni (fire), Varuna (water), and the rest of the Aryan pantheon.

The earliest text of the Aryan tribes was the *Rg Veda*, which became part of the scriptural text called the *Vedas*. This text was known to the Aryan tribes of India, as well as to the Aryan tribes in the Middle East, where they were known as the Persians and the Medes and later the Hittites. If we look at the *Rg Veda*, we can see the roots of Aryan thought, and we can see how this thought gave rise to the values of Western Civilization as the Aryans spread into the Indus Valley, the Middle East/Mesopotamia, Egypt, and into Northern Europe.

In their creation myth, the r'sis (priests) told a story which legitimized their role as spokesmen for the gods and also legitimized their political and economic behavior. In this story, the first priest Man offered his twin brother, the first king Yemo, (i.e., Twin) in sacrifice, along with the first ox. From Yemo's body the world was made. In the "Song of Purusha," quoted below, we see how the body was divided up and how the order of the universe came to be.

> *When they divided Purusha, how many pieces did they prepare?*
> *What was his mouth? What are his arms, thighs, and feet called?*
> *The priest was his mouth, the warrior was made from his arms;*

> *His thighs were the merchant, and the servant was born from his feet.*
> *The moon was born of his mind; of his eye, the sun was born; From his mouth, Indra and fire; from his breath, wind was born;*
> *From his naval there was the atmosphere; from his head, heaven was rolled*
>  *together;*
> *From his feet, the earth; from his ears, the directions.*[99]

From the above verse, we can determine a few things. Namely, the universe is no longer seen in the image of a Goddess, but rather of a God. Secondly, we can see that the priest class has gained ascendancy over the warrior class and they were in a position of power. This probably occurred as the priests learned their roles from the matriarchs of the old order. Thirdly, we can see the pecking order of the new class system emerge; specifically, the order was priests, warriors, merchants, and servants (slaves).

We can also determine that the ritual of sacrificing the *sacred king*, which was initiated in matriarchal times and served to connect the life force of the tribe with the Goddess, was now taken over by male priests and served to connect the life force of the tribe to a God. Sacrifice remained the most important of all Aryan rights. In the chapter on Indo-European religions in the *Encyclopedia of Religions* we are told: "Insofar as the first priest created the world through the performance of a sacrifice in which a man and an ox were the victims, so each subsequent priest re-created the cosmos by sacrificing men or cattle."[100]

In this ritual, the victim was dismembered and its material substance, like that of Purusa, was transformed into the corresponding parts of the universe. In the *Aitareya Brahmana* 2.6, we are provided with instructions for the sacrificial dismemberment of an animal victim.

*Lay his feet down to the north. Cause his eye to go to the sun.*
*Send forth his breath to the wind, his life force to the atmosphere,*
*His ears to the cardinal points, his flesh to the earth.*
*Thus, the priest places the victim in these worlds.*[101]

Like the matriarchs before them, the Aryan priests believed that without such sacrifice, the items of the material world, earth, air, sun, wind, etc. would become depleted. Only by sacrifice could they be replenished and life continue. Through sacrifice, the priests maintained the connection between their tribe and the universe, between man and god.

The Aryan religion was not altogether simplistic. It was subtle enough to invigorate a long line of r'sis' who justified Aryan behavior to their people and promoted their superiority over women and slaves for generation after generation. In their view of the cosmos, the questions surrounding the subject of death were of considerable concern. As the mystery of *life* had been the preoccupation of the matriarchs, the mystery of *death* became the preoccupation of the patriarchs. To overcome the people's fear of death, especially in battle, the r'sis taught that death was the last sacrifice that an individual could make to Indra, the war-god of the Aryans. In this instance, the warrior's own body became the offering. As such, his body would be transformed into the elements of the physical universe just as the sacred-king's body was transformed, as we saw in the "Song of Purusha". In the funeral hymn of the *Rg Veda*, we read:

*Your eye must go to the sun. Your soul must go to the wind.*
*You must go to the sky and the earth, according to what is right.*
*Go to the waters, if you are placed there.*
*You must establish the plants with your flesh. (Rg Veda 10.16.3)*

We can see that, in the progression of human thought, the sacrifice of the sacred-king was incorporated into the patriarchal ritual when the first male priest sacrificed his twin brother, the first king, to ensure the continual fruition of life. And now we see that each man was made sacred by his ability to reenact this event of creation and, in so doing, was able to identify himself with divinity. We will see this same theme in the religions of Mithraism, Judaism, Christianity, and Islam.

In Aryan myths, we find a scheme involving four great ages. The first age, the early Aryans believed, was pure and perfect, like the Garden of Eden. In the second, third, and fourth ages, however, human virtue and the order of the cosmos break down. At the end of the fourth age, there is an apocalyptic collapse followed by the creation of a new, pure, and regenerated world.[102] One of the features of the "end of the world" is the resurrection of the dead, whose bodies are made from the matter freed up when the universe falls apart.

Here we can see the roots of Western thought concerning death, Armageddon, and the resurrection of the dead into a better life.

The most cherished of the Aryan gods, Indra, was their war-god and the god of rain and thunderstorms. He wielded a thunderbolt. He was venerated as the god who led the Aryan raiding parties into battle. Going into battle, the men would invoke his assistance by pouring libations, getting drunk, and aspiring to states of ecstatic frenzy. Indra gained his stripes as a war-god in his first battle, in which he defeated the great serpent Vitra, the consort of the Great Goddess. With his muscular body and flowing white hair Indra provides, to this day, the image of God the Father in the western world. This is the image of God as immortalized in Michelangelo's ceiling of the Sistine Chapel in Rome. The praises of Indra are sung in the *Rg Veda*, the earliest of the *Vedas* and constitute almost twenty-five percent of the hymns.

Hymn XXXII from the *Rg Veda* describes how Indra derived his power by killing the great serpent (dragon) Vitra, the son of the Great Goddess (Danu). In the myth, the water that Vitra holds back is symbolic of the flow of knowledge possessed by the Goddess. The word *kine* means a herd of cows. The cows were originally the property of the Goddess. They were also the cows of the indigenous people of India, who the Aryans called Dasas (dark slaves). These slaves still worshipped the Goddess. The indigenous Dravidian people, who created one of the greatest agricultural civilizations on earth, had a subtle appreciation of the nature of reality and worshipped divine consciousness in the form of the Great Goddess. In order to establish their rule over the Dravidians, the Aryans had to defeat their Goddess. In this hymn from the *Rg Veda*, we are told how this was accomplished.

> 1 I WILL declare the manly deeds of Indra, the first that he achieved, the Thunder-wielder. He slew the Dragon, then disclosed the waters, and cleft the channels of the mountain torrents.
> 2 He slew the Dragon lying on the mountain: his heavenly bolt of thunder Tvastar fashioned. Like lowing kine in rapid flow descending the waters glided downward to the ocean.
> 3 Impetuous as a bull, he chose the Soma and in three sacred beakers drank the juices.
> Maghavan grasped the thunder for his weapon, and smote to death this firstborn of the dragons.
> 4 When, Indra, thou hadst slain the dragon's firstborn, and overcome the charms of the enchanters, Then, giving life to Sun and Dawn and Heaven, thou foundest not one foe to stand against thee.
> 5 Indra with his own great and deadly thunder smote into pieces Vrtra, worst of Vrtras.
> As trunks of trees, what time the axe hath felled them, low on the earth so lies the prostrate Dragon.
> 6 He, like a mad weak warrior, challenged Indra, the great impetuous many-slaying Hero.

*He, brooking not the clashing of the weapons, crushed—Indra's foe—the shattered forts in falling.*
*7 Footless and handless still he challenged Indra, who smote him with his bolt between the shoulders.*
*Emasculate yet claiming manly vigour, thus Vrtra lay with scattered limbs dissevered.*
*8 There as he lies like a bank-bursting river, the waters taking courage flow above him.*
*The Dragon lies beneath the feet of torrents which Vrtra with his greatness had encompassed.*
*9 Then humbled was the strength of Vrtra's mother: Indra hath cast his deadly bolt against her.*
*The mother was above, the son was under and like a cow beside her calf lay Danu.*
*10 Rolled in the midst of never-ceasing currents flowing without a rest for ever onward.*
*The waters bear off Vrtra's nameless body: the foe of Indra sank to during darkness.*
*11 Guarded by Ahi [Vitra] stood the thralls of Dāsas, the waters stayed like kine held by the robber. But he, when he had smitten Vrtra, opened the cave wherein the floods had been imprisoned.*
*12 A horse's tail wast thou when he, O Indra, smote on thy bolt; thou, God without a second, Thou hast won back the kine, hast won the Soma; thou hast let loose to flow the Seven Rivers.*
*13 Nothing availed him lightning, nothing thunder, hailstorm or mist which had spread around him: When Indra and the Dragon strove in battle, Maghavan [Indra] gained the victory forever.*
*14 Whom sawest thou to avenge the Dragon, Indra, that fear possessed thy heart when thou hadst slain him; That, like a hawk affrighted through the regions, thou crossedst nine-and-ninety flowing rivers?*

*15 Indra is King of all that moves and moves not, of creatures tame and horned, the Thunder-wielder. Over all living men he rules as Sovran, containing all as spokes within the felly.*¹⁰³

Among all the tribes of Aryans, we find a mythic battle ending with the slaying of a serpent-dragon on the part of a male deity. This is the central myth constructed to symbolize the death of matriarchy, represented by the Serpent, and the victory of patriarchy, which is represented by a male god. This transition is mythologized in Greek in the following conflicts: Zeus vs. Typhon, Kronos vs. Ophion, Apollo vs. Python, Heracles vs. the Hydra and Ladon, Perseus vs. Ceto, and Bellerophon vs. the Chimera.

In Germanic lore, we have the conflict between Thor vs. Jörmungandr, Sigurd vs. Fafnir, and Beowulf vs. the dragon.

In Persian and Zoroastrian mythology, we have Θraētaona, and later Kərəsāspa, vs. Aži Dahāka. In Slavic mythology, we have Perun vs. Veles and Dobrynya Nikitich vs. Zmey; in Romanian, Fat-Frumos vs. Zmeu; in Hittite, Tarhunt vs. Illuyanka.

There are also stories in other neighboring mythologies: Anu or Marduk vs. Tiamat in Mesopotamian mythology; Ra vs. Apep in Egyptian mythology; Baal or El vs. Lotan or Yam-Nahar in Levantine mythology; Yahweh or Gabriel vs. Leviathan or Rahab or Tannin in Jewish mythology; Michael the Archangel or Christ vs. Satan (in the form of a seven-headed dragon); and Saint George vs. the Dragon in Christian mythology. This central myth symbolized a clash between the patriarchal forces of order against chaos (represented by the serpent), and invariably the god or hero would win.¹⁰⁴

As the Aryans moved into the Indus Valley, we find hymns to Indra that not only exalt him for the destruction of the matriarchy, but also for the destruction of the indigenous people who still worshiped the Goddess:

*1 WITH sacrifice I purge both earth and heaven: I burn up great she-fiends who serve not Indra, Where throttled by*

> *thy hand the foes were slaughtered, and in the pit of death lay pierced and mangled.*
> *2 O thou who castest forth the stones crushing the sorceresses' heads, Break them with thy wide-spreading foot, with thy wide-spreading mighty foot.*
> *3 Do thou, O Maghavan, beat off these sorceresses' daring strength. Cast them within the narrow pit, within the deep and narrow pit.*
> *4 Of whom thou hast ere now destroyed thrice-fifty with thy fierce attacks. That deed they count a glorious deed, though small to thee, a glorious deed.*[105]

The worship of Indra clearly demonstrates that the motivation of the Aryan patriarchal tribes was not to gain spiritual insight but simply to conquer others in battle in order to steal their cattle and wealth and enslave them for work, as seen in Hymn X:

> *Easy to turn and drive away, Indra, is spoil bestowed by thee. Unclose the stable of the kine, and give us wealth O Thunder-armed*
> *The heaven and earth contain thee not, together, in thy wrathful mood.*
> *Win us the waters of the sky, and send us kine abundantly.*[106]

Hymn CII also reflects this motivation:

> *His arms win kine, his power is boundless in each act best, with a hundred helps, waker of battle's din is Indra: none may rival him in mighty strength. Hence, eager for the spoil the people call on him.*[107]

As seen in Hymn XXIX, it was Indra's habit to get drunk on soma and go out to do battle with the enemies of the Aryans:

1 O SOMA DRINKER, ever true, utterly hopeless though we be,
Do thou, O Indra, give us hope of beauteous horses and of kine,
In thousands, O most wealthy One.[108]

In Aryan society, the cattle raids "were raised to the status of a sacred act."[109] Rituals were created to invoke the assistance of Indra. In these rituals, the Aryan warriors became one with the gods by pouring libations, getting intoxicated, and working themselves up into a war frenzy. In such a state of mind, murder and plunder of their neighbors was justified and honored as fulfilling the desires of the gods. Whether the drink was mead, wine, or soma, its power resided in its capacity to increase the fighting spirit among the priests and the warriors, and—we might surmise—in its power to dull the senses to the slaughter that they would soon perpetrate.

In time, as the Aryans became more sophisticated due to contact with the more advanced Indian civilization of the Dravidians, Indra became more of a drunk and erratic in his behavior. As such, he began to lose favor. He was replaced by Shiva, who was worshiped as a God by both the Aryans and Dravidians. Shiva is remembered as the one who codified Tantric yoga and gave humanity the means to achieve Divinity. We will look at Shiva later as we uncover the roots of mysticism in human thought.

## The Invasion of the Indus Valley by the Aryans

The Aryan tribes living in the Caucasus were bordered on the west by the Black Sea and on the East by the Caspian Sea. They first moved south into the Middle East and then west into northern Europe. To the east, they fanned out across Afghanistan, Pakistan, Kashmir, and India (The Indus Valley). Here, the clash of cultures between the Dravidian matriarchal civilization and the Aryans nomadic tribes was especially dramatic. As the largest and most sophisticated of the matriarchal agricultural civilizations—larger than Egypt and Mesopotamia—the Indus Valley civilization provided the greatest contrast to the Aryan invasion in terms of gender, race, class, geography, history, economy, politics, religion, and spirituality. It was staggering in its impact and that initial clash and interpenetration continues to influence the people of India today.

As the Aryans came east in waves that lasted over hundreds of years, they first encountered Mehrgarh, a Neolithic culture dating back eighty-five hundred years ago. Mehrgarh lies on the Kacchi Plain of Balochistan, Pakistan, and is situated at the Bolan peak pass, which is one of the main routes connecting Iran, Afghanistan, Pakistan, and the Indus River valley. According to Catherine Jarrige of the Center for Archaeological Research, Indus Baluchistan at the Musée Guimet in Paris, "This area of rolling hills is thus located on the western edge of the Indus valley, where, around 2500 BCE, a large urban civilization emerged at the same time as those of Mesopotamia and the Ancient Egypt. For the first time in the Indian Subcontinent, a continuous sequence of dwelling-sites has been established from 7000 BCE to 500 BCE. . . ."[110]

After the bitter cold of the Caucasus, such an area must have seemed like paradise to the nomadic Aryan tribes. We are told that early Mehrgarh residents lived in mud brick houses, stored their grain in granaries, fashioned tools with copper ore, and lined their large basket containers with bitumen to carry liquids. They cultivated barley, einkorn, wheat, and dates and herded sheep, goats, and cattle. Residents from seventy-five hundred years ago were also involved in crafts such as flint knapping, tanning, bead production, and metal-working. Mehrgarh is probably the earliest known center of agriculture in South Asia and is now considered as a precursor to the Indus Valley Civilization.[111]

Over thirty-two thousand artifacts have been collected at this ancient site that covered about five hundred acres. Mehrgarh was matriarchal in its origin. Artifacts indicate manufacturing activity with glazed beads and terracotta figurines of females decorated with paint and diverse hairstyles and ornaments. Two burials were found in Period II (seventy-five to fifty-five hundred years ago) with a covering of red ochre on the body. The amount of burial goods decreased over time, becoming limited to ornaments, most with the burials of females. The oldest ceramic figurines in South Asia were found at Mehrgarh. They occur in all phases of the settlement and were prevalent even before pottery appeared. The earliest figurines are quite simple and do not show intricate features. However, they grow in sophistication with time and by six thousand years ago; they begin to show their characteristic hairstyles and typical prominent breasts. Many of the female figurines are holding babies and are interpreted as depictions of the "mother goddess".

All the figurines up to this period were female. Male figurines appear only from Period VII (forty-six hundred to four thousand years ago) and gradually become more numerous.[112]

The earliest Mother Goddess figurine unearthed in India, belonging to the Upper Paleolithic, has been carbon-dated to approximately 20,000 BCE.[113] Thousands of female statuettes dated as early as seventy-five hundred years ago have been discovered at Mehrgarh. Current archaeological and anthropological evidence suggests that the religion of the great Indus Valley Civilization was probably a direct predecessor of modern Shaktism. Shaktism is one of the four divisions of Hinduism in which the Great Goddess is worshipped as the ultimate Divinity.

Toward the end of the Mehrgarh period, the Indus Valley Civilization emerged.

It flourished in the basins of the Indus River and the now dried up Sarasvati River, which once coursed through northwest India and eastern Pakistan. At its peak, the Indus Civilization may have had a population of over five million people.[114] Over 1,056 cities and settlements had been found, of which ninety-six percent have been excavated.[115]

The largest of the destroyed cities excavated are Harappa and Mohenjo-daro. They were expertly planned with a grid pattern of wide boulevards. The cities contained indoor plumbing, public baths, central granaries, and multi-storied housing. The uniformity of weights and bricks in all localities was also extraordinary.[116]

Thick walls surrounded the cities. Many people lived in brick houses that had as many as three floors. Some houses even had bathrooms and toilets that connected to the world's first sewer system. An irrigation system of canals provided a reliable source of water for growing wheat and barley and for care of sheep, cattle, and goats that were raised by the people.

This testifies to the fact that, under matriarchy, the women had a highly advanced knowledge of mathematics and a sophisticated system of uniform weights and measures, suggesting that the cities had close communication with each other.

The people of the Indus River valley were apparently interested in cleanliness because excavators have uncovered evidence of combs, soaps, and medicine. There were also gravesites found with the remains of people whose teeth had been drilled, indicating an early awareness of dentistry.

It is clear that the Aryans did not build these cities. They lacked the capacity and interest to do so. The Aryan caste system is not in evidence anywhere in the remains of the cities, nor is there evidence of an administrative hierarchy. Archaeological records provide no immediate answers for a center of power or for depictions of people in power in Harappan society.

According to ethnologist Father Wilhelp Koppers, the matriarchy existed in India prior to the Neolithic period. Not surprisingly then, archaeologists found ample evidence from artifacts of the Great Goddess in the early Indus Valley as well.

In Harappa, a most unusual seal was found with a nude female, upside down, legs apart, and with a plant issuing from her vulva. On the left of the same face are two animal spirits, and between the spirits and the female is an undeciphered script. On the reverse side, the inscription is repeated and to its left are two human figures, one standing with a sickle-shaped knife in the right hand and the latter seated on the ground with hands raised in supplication. The man who discovered the seal, Sir John Marshall, interpreted the figures as the man with the knife and the woman kneeling in supplication.[117] It is more likely, (because the gender cannot be determined), that this standing figure was a female, and that this image depicts the ancient ritual of the sacrifice of the sacred king.

The evidence of a script, although not yet deciphered by archaeologists, indicates that the script was probably a combination of Dravidian and Austric Munda. The Aryans possessed no script of their own at the time of the invasion.

The Indus Valley civilization was one of the earliest mother-ruled agricultural civilizations and possibly the highest developed. Because of the enormous wealth due to agriculture and trade, it is most likely that the city was going through the fratriarchal period at the time of the Aryan invasion. What we do know about Harappa was that when the city collapsed, it was amidst disease and trauma. Human skeletal remains demonstrated some of the highest rates of injury (15.5 percent) found in south Asian prehistory. Furthermore, rates of cranio-facial trauma and infection increased through time. Bio-archaeologists also found that some individuals and communities at Harappa were excluded from access to basic resources like health and safety. This was not a feature of matriarchal society where wealth was held communally. It is rather a distinct feature of patriarchal societies worldwide.[118] What scientists found was the result of invasion.

Mohenjo-daro was another great city of the Indus Valley Civilization. It was built around forty-six hundred years ago.

Numerous artifacts found in the excavation include seated and standing figures, copper and gold, stone tools, carved seals, balance scales and weights, jewelry, and children's toys. A particular bronze statuette dubbed the "Dancing Girl", made about forty-five hundred years ago, has fascinated archaeologists since its discovery by Mortimer Wheeler in 1926. Wheeler described the statuette in these words: "She's about fifteen years old I should think, not more, but she stands there with bangles all the way up her arm and nothing else on. A girl for the moment, perfectly confident of herself and the world. There's nothing like her I think in the world."[119]

Another archaeologist, Gregory Possehl, said of the statuette, "We may not be certain that she was a dancer, but she was good at what she did and she knew it."[120] A small clue of this nature lets us know that women were still respected and held a place of high esteem in the world during the time of Mohenjo-daro.

Another interesting artifact is a seated male soapstone figure that archaeologists dubbed the "Priest-King." While there is no evidence that priests or monarchs ruled Mohenjo-daro, this figure could well indicate a male authority figure. If so, we can determine that he was performing his role within the context of the matriarchy or fratriarchy during the transition that was occurring at the time.[121] It is also possible, according to Joseph Campbell, that, because of its appearance, the figure originated in Sumeria and was brought to Mohenjo-daro.[122]

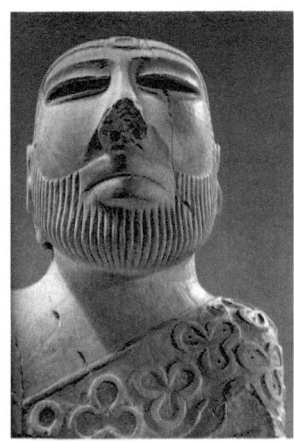 

Another artifact that caused a lot of attention is a great seal that bears an image of a seated, cross-legged figure surrounded by animals. The figure has been interpreted by some scholars as a yogi and by others as a three-headed "proto-Shiva" as "Lord of Animals" (Pashupati).[123] If this is a seal with an image of Shiva on it, this would indicate that Shiva existed as early as seven thousand years ago. This is close to the time in which Shrii P. R. Sarkar says that Shiva lived and at the time the Aryans had already entered India. Shiva is significant in that he was the first God-realized human being in history.

The Indus River Valley cities traded with distant foreign cultures. Archaeologists have found jewelry made in Harappa as far away as Mesopotamia. Traders also sold cotton cloth and hardwood from the teak trees that grew in the valley.

When the Aryans rolled into the Indus Valley, they came on horseback and chariot. At the time, the chariort was the greatest war weapon invented. There had been a four-wheel chariot, invented by the Sumerians, with solid wheels that was drawn by donkeys, but by the time of the invasion, the Aryans had invented a horse drawn chariot that was easier to maneuver because of spoked wheels revolving freely on their axis.[124]

Groups of skeletons of men, women, and children left lying with sword and ax cuts were found in the topmost level of Mohenjo-daro indicating a raiding party had killed and moved through. Apparently the Aryans, whom Joseph Campbell calls "polygamous, patriarchal, proud of their genealogies, tent dwellers, filthy and tough," had no interest in cities. Once they destroyed them, there were no more cities in the Indus Valley for a thousand years.[125]

Where did the Aryans live, if not in the cities? Several sites around the cities indicate squatters living in low-grade shoddy shacks upon the ruins of the cities.[126]

In the *Rg Veda*, there are several references to destroying forts and fortified cities. The city residents who lived through the invasions were mostly women and children, who were taken as slaves. The men were massacred because the Aryans did not yet know how to enslave them.

According to Shrii P. R. Sarkar, the Aryans entered the Indus Valley (Afghanistan, Pakistan, Kashmir, and India in several stages). During the first stage they reached the land of the seven rivers or Saptasindhu: the Sind (now called Indus), the Shatadru, Irávatii (Ravi), Vipáshá (Biás), Chandrabhagá (Chenub), Vitastá (Jhalúm), and Kabul. Along with the land of the seven rivers, they also colonized the kingdom of Shivi, which is most likely the ancient name for Sindh in present day Pakistan.

In the second stage, the Aryans reached Haritdhánya, a state of north-central India west of New Delhi. In the third stage, they reached the confluence of the Ganges and Yamuna rivers. During the age of the Mahábhárata (600 BC), this area was known as the kingdom of Shúrasena with its capital at Mathura; its king was Kam☒sa and afterwards Lord Krśńa, who was another God-realized master in Indian history.[127]

In the fourth stage, they reached the kingdom of Káshii in Uttar Pradesh, close to the present city of Allahabad. When they attempted to move further east towards Magadha and Videha, they faced great resistance. Nonetheless, they managed to conquer Mithila (east of Bihar) and Magadha, and then they proceeded towards Ráŕh (roughly between Ranchi and Kolkata) where they met with insurmountable opposition. By this time, the indigenous people had learned how to fight. There is also evidence that they used dogs and wolves to attack the Aryans.

The Aryan advance came to a standstill at the threshold of the kingdom of Káshiirájya (Varanasi or Benares). They tried to incorporate Mithila, but in the end they could not rule it. The word *magadh* means "a population which is opposed to the Vedic system." *Maga* means "opposed to the *Vedas*" and *dha* means "one who abides by." Ráŕh, which was located on the eastern border of Magadh, remained untouched by the Aryans. Over time, however, as the Aryans consolidated their hold over northern India, their caste system eventually entered Magadh and also Rarh, to a lesser extent. Nonetheless, the fact that the Aryans were slow to penetrate this part of India, there culture was less impactful on the people there, and the influence of Shiva and Tantrik yoga, to this day, remains stronger in this area.[128]

## Slavery and Racism

It was not difficult for the healthy, almost invincible Aryans to conquer most of northern India. In doing so, the victorious Aryans treated the vanquished inhabitants as slaves. After major battles, they would kill the men of the conquered communities and enslave the women and children. While they tried to prevent interbreeding with the slave women, it was impossible and the Caucasoid race became mixed like all other races. The mixture of races has historically been of little significance beyond its use as a device for political exploitation.

The Aryans conquered and enslaved local peoples, most of whom were darker and smaller than themselves. The most archaic word for slave is dasa (dark). This behavior of enslaving smaller and physically weaker people become the modus operandi of the Aryan tribes.

Today we can see the Caucasian patriarchs' long history of enslavement of people of color. Even today, Caucasians in so-called "civilized societies" like the United States and Europe still believe they have the right to dominate people of color, using them to do their bidding. In the beginning, the Aryan women and children were the slaves or property of the males. Now the women and children of the indigenous people also became slaves. And just as the males felt it necessary to humiliate and dominate women through brute force, laws, and myths, so they felt it necessary to do the same to people of color. Thus, we see the origins of white supremacy and racism in this world and its link to slavery.

Because racism is a socio-sentiment based on one's conception of race and has nothing to do with one's humanity, especially one's mental or spiritual capacity, it is worth saying a word about race at this time. For it is here in northern India that the deep-seated programming of the white racism finds its earliest expression. Races are defined by certain bodily features that develop due to the impact of environmental and cultural features.

Shrii P. R. Sarkar speaks of four main races that evolved early in human history as a result of environment differences. Anthropologists call these races Caucasoid, Mongoloid, Negroid, and Australoid. There is, however, no such thing as a pure race due to a hundred thousand years of sexual relations between people all over the earth. In fact, current DNA can trace the entire human race back to a Negroid mother who lived in Africa about 200,000 years ago. Scientists call her *Mitochondrial Eve*.[129]

According to Shrii P. R. Sarkar, the Aryans, who were the Nordic branch of the Caucasoid race, moved west from the Caucasus to the Danube Valley and then to central and western Europe. They also advanced south settling in Iran (a cognate of Aryan), Syria, Palestine, Egypt, North Africa, Spain, and along the Mediterranean coast. They spread out from western France to the British Isles. To the east, they spread to Afghanistan and the Indus Valley (Pakistan, Kashmir, and India).

The Mongolian homeland was China. Later, they crossed the Arctic Ocean to the Bering Strait and moved into North America. They could not move westward because of the obstruction of high mountains in Asia. So they advanced eastward and southward and reached Burma, Siam (Thailand), Indochina, Sumatra, Java, Borneo, the Philippines, and Japan and joined with the original inhabitants of those places who were the Austrics.

The Negroid race lived near the equator in Africa and New Guinea, near the southern coast of the Indian Ocean. Their descendants, the Austrics, are found in South India, the Andaman Islands, the Malayan Peninsula, and the Philippines. Shrii P. R. Sarkar considers the Dravidians to be a combination of Austrics and Negroes.

The Caucasoid had three branches, the Nordic, Alpine, and Mediterranean. The Alpines and the Mediterraneans produced the Sumerian, Egyptian, and Hellenic civilizations. The Nordics (Aryans) and the Dravidians were responsible for the Indus Valley civilization. And the Mongolians produced the Chinese and Japanese civilizations. The Mongolians also formed the base for the Native Americans, who built up the American civilizations before the arrival of the Europeans. The Negroes created civilizations in Africa. The Austrics were the indigenous populations of Malaysia, Philippines, East India, Indonesia, and Australia.

Some genealogists also speak of a Semitic race. Semites would include various ancient and modern peoples originating in southwestern Asia, including the Acadians, Canaanites, Phoenicians, Hebrews, and Arabs.

There has been a historical mixture of the blood of these different races, which led to more "races" being labeled by anthropologists as well as by political opportunists. For example, in India all the four prominent races—the Caucasoid, the Mongoloid, Australoid and Negroid—have become thoroughly mixed. And so it is in the rest of the world today. There is no such thing as a pure race and, even if this were the case, what would be the advantage of pursuing racial purity? It goes against human nature. Statements by people like Adolph Hitler that, "the Aryans are not to be ruled but to rule," is nothing but arrogance, ignorance, and chauvinism. The modern Germans, as with all people are a mixed race. The talk of "pure blood" of race is meaningless. All blood is pure. Racism, the belief that one's "race" is superior to others, has no basis in fact, nor is race a determinant of one's humanity. Racism is rather a throwback in history when human groups were fearfully coming together for the first time for various reasons: to fight collectively against the forces of nature, to conquer and expand territory, or to share a common religion, a geographical proximity, reciprocal trade, or cultural exchanges.

Ultimately, close association culminated in sexual relations and marital bonds across races. Sometimes many small groups were fused into a new "race" through inter-racial marriages. For instance, in South America, as a result of constant intermingling of the blood of African slaves, the Europeans, and the indigenous people, a new race has emerged. Similarly, in Colombia and Mexico, a new Mestizo community has come into being as a result of interracial marriages between the Europeans and Native Americans. That is why it is meaningless to consider one's race superior to others. The outdated socio-sentiment of racism is crumbling today as a newly awakened humanity looks forward to one universal human society.

External differences among social groups cannot alter our basic human traits—love and affection, pleasure and pain, and hunger and thirst. These basic biological instincts and mental propensities exist in human beings of all complexions, in all countries, and in all ages. An illiterate, half-naked tribal mother in a primitive village bears the same deep maternal affection for her young child as a well-educated mother in New York City. Shrii P. R. Sarkar tells us:

The subterranean flow of love and affection exists in all hearts alike. Every person cries out in pain, everyone feels pleasure when there are occasions of joy and happiness. In different geographical, cultural, social and other environments the lifestyles of different human groups may vary – a few special psychic traits of some of those groups may assert themselves – but fundamentally their mental existence flows along the same channels of ideas and consciousness. Containing the same cosmic momentum and under the same cosmic inspiration, they all have set out for a tryst with the same destiny.[130]

## The Aryan Caste System

While modern human beings may understand the damage caused by racism in the world, during the time of the Aryan invasion, this obviously was not the case. Racism was used as a means by the Aryans to control their slaves and bolster their self-pride. The Aryan intellectuals also instituted a system of social stratification (i.e., a class structure) to perpetuate their dominance over the entire society. The ruling class, of course, consisted of the Brahmins (r'sis). They imposed their religious rituals, dogmas, and rules on the people in order to exploit them and to ensure themselves more wealth and power. The second class were the Ksattriyans or the warriors. The third class were the Vaeshyas or merchants. At the bottom were the Shudras or the laboring masses. Below these classes were the slaves. After a time, the Aryans granted some of their slaves shudra status. The rest remained the *untouchables*. This class system, called the *caste system*, still exists in India today. It is the most venal, destructive class system on earth because one's caste prohibits social mobility and is defined by iron-clad rules and limited opportunities. The caste in which one is born is the caste in which one dies.

As the complexity of Aryan-Dravidian society evolved over millennia, it was difficult to maintain such a strict control over the vast, multi-lingual population. Yet, even as late as 1932, an attempt was made to provide the general characteristics of the caste system in India.

G. S. Ghurye said the following descriptors of caste could be applied across the country, although he acknowledged that there were regional variations on the general theme:

> strict segmentation of society, with the various groups being rigidly defined and membership determined by birth;
>
> a hierarchical system that defines a ranking place for all of the castes;
>
> limited choice of occupation, which is enforced within a caste as well as by other castes (a caste might follow more than one traditional occupation but its members would nonetheless be constrained to that range);
>
> acceptance of the general practice of endogamy (marrying only in one's caste), and in some situations hypergamy (marrying into a higher caste) (Endogamy applies to the various sub-groups within a caste itself, preventing marriage between the sub-groups and sometimes imposing an additional geographical constraint, such as one can only marry a person from the same gotra and the same place);
>
> restrictions on dietary and social interactions that define who could consume what and from whom (as with marriage arrangements, these restrictions apply at sub-caste level, not merely at the caste level);

physical segregation; for example, in villages (this is accompanied by limitations on movement and access, including to religious and educational areas and to basic facilities such as supplies of water; again, this segregation applies at sub-caste level as well as at the higher level).[131]

The ruling class has succeeded in imposing severe control over people's inter-relations, marriage, diet, travel, segregation, occupation, etc. The caste system remains especially resistant to change because it is buttressed by an understanding of social psychology, as well as by the exploitive religious dogma of the r'sis, who in Hinduism represent the voice of God. As Shrii P. R. Sarkar tells us: "Religious dogma gave new meaning to the concept of life after death. People were taught that they were poor because they had committed sinful acts in their past lives and that they were rich because their past deeds were virtuous.... If you analyze each and every aspect of life which has been infected by religious dogma, you will find that the advocates of dogma are always motivated by the psychology of exploitation."[132]

The caste system in India provides a clear danger signal when it comes to typecasting. It will require extreme caution, therefore, when we utilize the knowledge of social psychologies as a tool to create social revolution. A strong antidote to the tendency of rulers to typecast people into a static caste system is to ensure that revolutionary leaders incorporate all social psychologies into their own personality to better understand and serve all people regardless of class. By social psychology, we mean the methods by which human beings either gain power in life or do not. For example, a person or group may have power due to the use of physical force (warrior), mental force (intellectual), or control of money (merchant). The masses of people, however, have never been able to overcome the forces against them and they are called the laboring masses. We will talk more about the significance of social psychology and how it gives rise to social classes, in greater detail in Book Two. In the meantime, it is critical that we understand that one's social psychology may change according to condition and, indeed, must change if we are to advance as human beings.

To lock the human mind into a caste prison is dogmatism of the most destructive type. Like sexism and racism, everyone should fight against classism.

One last observation can be made about the longevity of Aryan imperialism. Between 1860 and 1920, the British imperialists made use of the caste system in their divide and conquer strategy to rule India. They fortified the old system by granting administrative jobs and senior appointments only to the upper castes.[133]

With the onset of patriarchy, human beings were introduced to three elements, which continue today as a foundation for the social programming of western civilization. These are sexism/misogyny, racism, and classism. Having observed the conditions in which these sentiments arose, we must ask ourselves whether they still serve a purpose in moving us forward as a society. If not, we should do everything in our power to eliminate them from our thoughts and feelings because the time that we have to get organized as a human society to solve our current economic and environmental problems is becoming shorter.

# Lord Shiva and the Birth of Mysticism

WHEN THEY ARRIVED IN the Indus Valley, the Aryans introduced their religion to the Dravidians. These were the Vedas. At the time of their arrival, the Vedas were not written down because the Aryans had no script. It was through the mix of Aryan and Dravidian cultures that the Sanskrit script was invented. Based on the language of Sanskrit, the Aryan tribes, who would later settle in the Middle East and Europe, would share a common "Indo-European" language.

From the time that the *Rg Veda* was first written down around four thousand years ago, until the time of Pānini who wrote the first book on Sanskrit grammar about twenty-four hundred years ago, the development of Sanskrit can also be observed in other written Vedic texts. These include the *Samaveda, Yajurveda, Atharvaveda, Brahmanas, Upanishads*, and *Puranas*.[134] These religious texts constitute the foundation of Aryan Hinduism.

As the centuries rolled on, the integration between the Aryan and Dravidian cultures increased and Sanskrit underwent change. Different regional languages came into existence. Despite the tremendous differences between the Aryans and the Dravidians, the indigenous people became more accepting of the Aryans, while the Aryans assimilated the conquered people's higher culture. Of special significance is the Aryan adaptation of the spiritual practices of the indigenous people. By the time the *Upanishads* had evolved, the teachings reflect knowledge of *Parama Puruśa* or Supreme Consciousness. "Upa" means *near*, "ni" means *closely* and "śad" means to *sit*. So "Upaniśad" means that which leads us close to the Supreme Entity.[135] This is clearly the result of the merger of the Vedas with the Tantra of the indigenous people. Perhaps no individual has influenced this process more than Lord Shiva who was responsible for taking the Dravidian religious practice of Tantra and elevating it to a spiritual science. It was the integration of the Aryan religion, myths, stories, and laws with the spiritual science of Tantra that gave rise to Hinduism as it exists today.

The entire structure of Hinduism, which is the oldest extant mainstream religion, is, in fact, a merger of four religions, *Shaktism, Vaishnavism, Shaivism,* and *Smartism*. Shaktism has its roots in the matriarchy and worships the Great Goddess, often in the form of Kali. The origins of Shaktism, as we have seen, preceded the advent of the Aryans. Vaishnavism has its roots in the *Rg Veda* of the Aryans where Vishnu is mentioned as the supreme deity. Smartism derives from a particular Aryan priest class that specializes in the *smriti* (i.e., the remembered texts which include Aryan law). They worship the Supreme as Shiva, Shakti, Vishnu, and also Ganesha and Surya. Shaivism is directly based on the Tantrik teachings of Shiva and the worship of him as the highest divinity. Today, in fact, all branches of Hinduism worship Shiva as the Divine entity.

According to Shrii P.R. Sarkar, Shiva was not a fabricated god, but rather a real flesh and blood human being, who lived about seven thousand years ago after the Aryans had already entered India and the relationship between the Aryans and Dravidians was still one of great animosity.

It is worth learning a little about Shiva because more than any other human being, he gave shape to Eastern Civilization. He also provided the West with a mystical impulse that appeared in the mystery religions of the Hellenic civilization and in Buddhism, which influenced the Jewish Essenes in the Middle East. Even the yoga trend in the United States today, unbeknownst to most people, owes its origin to Shiva. Yet American yoga, for the most part, is only a health fad that barely skims the surface of the science of yoga as introduced by Shiva.

The impact of Shiva on Eastern Civilization is incalculable. He grew up in a Tantric culture that was part of the Dravidian matriarchy. *Tantra* means to liberate the mind from bondage. Shiva took this nascent religious philosophy and turned it into a spiritual science (i.e., Tantric Yoga). *Yoga* means to yoke the individual consciousness with the Divine Consciousness. During his lifetime, Shiva bewildered everyone with his accomplishments. He literally became the living God of both the Aryans and the Dravidians, despite the fact that their worldviews and lifestyles were diametrically opposed to each other. After his lifetime, it became impossible for subsequent religions of the East to gain any legitimacy unless they incorporated Shiva, his teachings and, spiritual practices into their pantheon.

Because of Shiva, around five thousand years ago, the Aryan r'sis replaced Indra, their drunken war god, and their pantheon of forces of nature with a concept of Saguna Brahma and Nirguna Brahma. This is undoubtedly the subtlest philosophical conception of Divinity ever conceived by human beings. *Saguna Brahma* means Qualified Consciousness (i.e., Consciousness as expressed in form—the universe). Nirguna Brahma means Consciousness without qualities (i.e., Absolute Consciousness unexpressed in forms). The r'sis also made reference to Purusha and Prakriti or, as they are better known, Shiva and Shakti.[136] Purusha and Prakriti or Shiva and Shakti constitute the initial Cosmic Duality that exists within the Absolute Consciousness. Usually Purusha (Shiva) is considered to be the cognitive principle (i.e., Consciousness itself), while Prakriti (Shakti) is considered to be the operative principle (i.e., the force or energy that binds consciousness into form and gives rise to the universe). We will discuss this spiritual theory in greater depth in Book 2 on Ideology. Let us be content at this time to simply acknowledge that as early as seven thousand years ago, in northern India, Lord Sadashiva introduced human beings to the science of spiritual liberation.

The Aryans believed that Shiva was a human representation of God consciousness. He was more than a god conjured up to represent some force of nature or principle of being; rather he was a man who walked the earth and whose wisdom and contribution to humanity was so great, that they attributed Divine status to him. It was Shiva, in his embodiment of divine consciousness, who introduced spiritual science to humanity.

## Shiva's Legacy

The teachings of Shiva have formed the esoteric core of Eastern thought for the last seven thousand years. Shiva, who is normally pictured dressed in a tiger skin, riding on an ox, carrying a trident, having snakes around his neck, and possessing long matted locks, has come down through the ages identified with drunkenness, frenzied sexuality, fertility rituals, human sacrifices, phallic worship, yoga, esoteric mysteries, and the highest form of Divinity. In religious mythology, he has been coupled with multiple goddesses and fathered innumerable gods and goddesses. Shiva, like Dionysus for the Greeks, was the god of magical power, intoxication, ecstatic sexuality, and transcendence, who initiated us into communion with the creative forces of life.

In India, during the Post-Shiva Tantra period following his death, Shiva was incorporated into all the Vedic texts. He was also accepted into the religion of the Jains and the Buddhists, where he became associated with phallic worship. People practiced phallic worship to increase their populations. After the Jains and the Buddhists, Shiva was incorporated into the Shiva cult of the Paoranik Age (fifth and sixth century AD) where he is called Iishvara.

The Natha Cult resulted from a synthesis between Buddhist tantra and the Paoranik Shiva cult. Here Shiva was called Natha.

The masters of this cult were considered avatars of Shiva. After their deaths, people made idols of them and worshipped them in the temples as incarnations of Shiva.[137]

The great personality of Shiva penetrated the entire religious history of India. But his influence was not limited to the upper stratum of society. Shiva belongs to everyone. He is worshipped by the common people—the shudras and untouchables—but not just as a religious figure, a deity of some scripture or god of some priest class. People could not live without loving him. This Shiva is called Laokik Shiva.

A simple poem, by Rabindranath Tagore, immortalizes the people's sentiment about Shiva.

> You were there in the play of my childhood dolls,
> You were there in my morning worship of Shiva.
> I have broken and rebuilt your image again and again.
> You are seated on the altar with my deity;
> When I do His worship, I worship You as well.
> You are the supreme goal of all gods,
> Eternal, the oldest of the old.
> You are as old as the morning radiance.
> Emeriini from the origin of infinity
> In an eternal flow of bliss,
> In expressions ever-new,
> You are shining in my heart.[138]

After seven thousand years, the people have not forgotten Shiva, neither the educated nor uneducated, neither the upper castes nor the untouchables. All people, despite their caste, community, or education surrender before the love of Shiva and have a saying: "I totally surrender myself to You, You are my ultimate refuge, You are the culminating point of the journey of my life."

As the image of Shiva went through the metamorphosis of history and changed into every form of mythical god to suit whatever purpose was required, we cannot forget that he was a real human being who reached super-human proportions by virtue of the fact that he was the first God-realized human being to walk this planet. Shiva was to the East, what Jesus became to the West.[139]

Shrii P. R. Sarkar, in his book *Namah Shivaya Shantaya*, analyzes the various attributes of Shiva and how his location in the pantheons of different religions came about. It is fascinating to see how this happened.[140]

Yet even more fascinating is Shrii P. R. Sarkar's description of Shiva the man and his accomplishments, which have awed and endeared him to people through the millennia. There is no historical record of the man Shiva because script had not yet been invented during his time. Yet Shrii P.R. Sarkar, as a Tantrik master whose knowledge also appears unlimited, has revealed to us the greatness of the God-man Shiva.

## The Meaning of "Shiva"

Shiva was a simple man who grew up in a Tantric environment, but who was also familiar with the Vedas. The name Shiva has three meanings. The first meaning is *welfare*. People say that Shiva serves people in five ways. These are depicted in Indian art showing Shiva with five faces. Of the two on the left, one causes excruciating torture and the other the shedding of tears. The face in the middle is calm and tranquil. The faces on the right express tenderness and love. Thus, Shiva is both severe and tender in his role as promoter of welfare.

The second meaning of Shiva is "cognition in its zenith state." Shiva means Parama Purusha, the Absolute Consciousness. The third meaning is Sadashiva, the name of the man who was born on the earth and who used his whole life to advance the cause of universal welfare.

Shiva was born at a time when the matriarchy was in decline, but the matrilineal order was still practiced. Different clans lived on different hills or high ground that they called *gotras*. People were identified according to which gotra they belonged. While the gotra during the matriarchy was ruled by a wise woman, during the Aryan-introduced patriarchy, it was ruled by a r'si or priest. As was typical during the age of patriarchy, one gotra was always fighting with one or more other gotras. Shiva told his followers not to divide themselves into gotras but to eat and drink together as members of one human family. This universal family the people called Shivagotra. In this way, Shiva introduced universality into the minds of the people and fought against narrow group sentiments. This, of course, put him at odds with those who benefitted from maintaining their base of power by promoting an *us-vs-them* mentality.

During the Vedic age, when women were treated as mere commodities of enjoyment, Shiva did not forget the great contribution women made to the evolution of human society, including language, agriculture, mathematics, astronomy, the concept of time, the first civilization, etc. He also held women in the deepest respect for their development of the spiritual practices of Tantra.

Shrii P. R. Sarkar said this about the origins of Tantra:

> Tantra is certainly older than the Vedas. Just as the shlokas or mantras of the Vedas were handed down from guru to disciple in a genealogical tradition, the Tantra sádhaná of the Mongolo-Dravidian society was handed down from guru to disciple hereditarily. The Vedas are theoretical full of ritualistic ceremonies and formalisms. It would be incorrect to regard Tantra as a more recent version of those Vedic rituals. Tantra's esoteric practices had long been known in the society of sádhakas (spiritual practitioners).[141]

Shiva understood intimately the rightful status of women and demanded that women be honored and respected as mothers, as they had been during the matriarchy. Consequently, we find, even today in places like Bengal and southern India, men share the custom of addressing unknown women as *ma'* or mother.

## The Gifts of Shiva

### A Marriage of Mutual Respect

Shrii P. R. Sarkar credits Shiva with creating the first marriage based on mutual respect and service. We have seen how marriage was a relationship based on male ownership of the wife. In the days of Shiva, there were also polygamous relationships of where unmarried men and women had multiple partners. A woman could have more than one husband (rare) and a man could have more than one wife—own more than one wife. Shiva had three wives—Parvatii, an Aryan woman, Gaunga, a Mongolian woman, and Kalii, a Negroid-Austric woman. He married these three distinct women to counter racism and classism. Shiva's system of marriage is known as *Shaeva Viva'ha*. The husband does not buy and enslave his wife; rather, the husband and wife equally share responsibility for their marriage, without consideration of caste or gotra. Shiva also told the men that if their wives were incapable of earning a living due to pregnancy, childcare, or circumstantial pressure, it was the responsibility of the husband to support her. This rule made it easier for the women to raise the children, because they did not have to worry about feeding and clothing them. As the children became older, the fathers took on direct responsibility for their care and maintenance.

Often times, because it was not easy to know the fathers of children, children would know only their mothers. Since the mother had so many responsibilities in assuming both the roles of mother and father, the time to nurture her children was compromised. Thus, quite often, the children were deprived of motherly love and affection and would not develop the finer sensibilities and sweetness of human interaction. We see this is true today as well.

Shiva was the first person to marry a woman for the purpose of mutual love and support. Before him, no man married a woman for any other purpose other than to own her and her children. No male would take any kind of household responsibility. Shiva encouraged women to seek the welfare of their husbands and to make a happy home.

People also addressed Shiva as the first father (a'dipita'). It did not mean he was the first married man. Rather, it meant that out of his deep love and compassion, he provided a safe shelter, not only to human beings, but also to animals. As the protector of animals, he was worshipped as Pashupati. Shiva protected all animals by giving them food to eat, warmth in cold weather, and consolation in sorrow, and by making them realize the warm feeling of existence.[142]

Shiva provided the impetus for a great leap forward for humanity by generating a loving environment and a social atmosphere of peace and happiness. By being around Shiva, people began to realize that they were human beings. Under Shiva's guidance, they learned to live their lives in harmony and rhythm. This is why Shiva is called the first father of the human race, and why the common people love him even to this day.

### The Octave, Mudra, and Dance

Shiva is also credited with giving other great gifts to humanity. For example, at the time of the *Rg Veda*, people understood rhythm or meter when it came to chanting, but they did not understand scale or pitch. Shiva invented the octave. This was no small feat considering that all music today is based on the octave. In addition, Shiva established harmony between rhythm and dance and added the *mudra* to them.[143] A mudra is a hand gesture or bodily posture used to convey feeling. Shiva realized that each gesture affects different glands in the body and therefore affects people's minds accordingly. He created dance for the explicit purpose of elevating people spiritually. This legacy can still be seen today in the Classical Dance of India. Shiva also created a dance called Tandava for the purpose of turning men into spiritual warriors. When we see statuettes of Shiva dancing as Nataraj, this is the dance that he is performing. Again, by considering the impact of movement on the glandular system, Shiva realized that when the dancer remains above the ground, he derives much benefit, when he touches the ground these benefits are assimilated into the body. Thus, Tandava is a jumping dance.

## Medical Science

Shiva brought order to whatever he touched. Another of his accomplishments was the creation of Tantra-oriented medicine (vaedyak shastra). Ever since human beings have been alive, they were familiar with some kinds of medicine. Even animals will eat certain plants or rub their bodies against certain trees or plants when they are sick. During the Vedic age, the Aryans brought their own medicine to India. It was called Ayurveda, the Vedic School of medicine. It included plants of medicinal value, but the medicinal value of these plants was usually discovered accidentally and there was no system. Shiva gave it form. He also introduced dissection, surgical operations, stitching, and other practices that the Aryans would not perform because they would not touch dead bodies, especially those that belonged to shudras or untouchables. Therefore, they deprived themselves of learning about the body. Shiva's system not only benefitted India, but also gave rise to developments in alchemy, chemistry, and the medicine of Central Asia.

## Care for Plants and Animals

People have long believed that this world is for human enjoyment only, so the existence of all the plants and animals in the world is merely to provide objects of enjoyment for human beings. Out of this human ignorance, people do not realize that plants and animals also have hopes and aspirations. They too have an intense desire to live. Yet, we believe that their pains and pleasures and their affectionate family or community lives are simply without value. This defective philosophy has made people ruthlessly violent, even more dangerous than blood thirsty tigers that kill only to preserve their physical existence. Human beings kill animals mostly out of greed and sport.[144]

This defective philosophy was certainly in vogue among the Aryans at the time of their invasion of the Indus Valley. In fact, the Aryans held this worldview in regard to other humans as well. It is well known that at the time of the Aryan invasion, mutual relations between the original inhabitants of India (Austrico-Mongolo-Negroids) and the Aryans, were by no means cordial. The Aryans had deep-rooted contempt for the indigenous people of India and called them *asuras* (monsters), *dánavas* (demons), or *dásas* (slaves). The Aryans did not accept the indigenous people into their society; rather, they declared them to be outcasts. But these ancient Indian people of Austrico-Mongolo-Negroid blood had their own civilization and culture. They were, in fact, an evolved people who had already developed the sciences of Tantra and medicine.

The story is told in the Indian epic, the *Mahabharata*, that Párvatii, the wife of Shiva, was the daughter of the Aryan King Daksha, who ruled in the Himalayan regions. Many people were hopeful that after the marriage between Párvatii and Shiva, the relations between the Aryans and the Dravidians would improve. Unfortunately, the relationship became more strained. Parvati's father Daksha and the Aryans continued their slanderous campaign against Shiva, and to humiliate Shiva, they held a sacrificial ceremony to which Shiva was not invited. Párvatii went to attend the ceremony, and, unable to bear the insults to her dear husband, immolated herself in the Aryan's sacrificial fire. Her last words were:

"I am a follower of Sadáshiva, the brilliance of whose divine presence outshines even the dazzling brilliance of the jewels of

Kuvera's treasury; whose unmatched dexterity in creation excels even that of the creator Brahmá Himself; whose unequalled love surpasses even that of the dissolver Maheshvara Himself; in whose loving shelter not only humans, but also animals and plants, feel absolutely secure. You certainly know this. I cannot bear this insult to Shiva any longer. Stop, Father, stop!"[145]

In referring to Lord Shiva as Sadáshiva, she had reminded the gathering that Shiva was the protector of all beings, including all plants and animals. Shiva is still remembered today as Pashupati, the Lord of Animals,[146] because animals would come to Shiva when they were disturbed or fearful. Shiva always made them feel peaceful again. After her self-immolation, the relations between the Aryans and the non-Aryans were said to have improved.[147]

## Spiritual Science: Tantric Yoga

Shiva's greatest contribution to India and to all of humanity was the systemization of the spiritual theory and practice of Tantra yoga. Tantrik yoga is based on the knowledge of color and sound vibrations, both internally and externally. For example, in the different energy centers (chakras) of the human body, there are different types of gland and sub-glands. From these different glands, hormones are secreted and these hormones control the body as well as one's psychic propensities. There are fifty basic propensities of the mind and the controlling points of these propensities are located in the seven energy centers or chakras of the human body. Each chakra emits a color and a sound. The inseparable association of these colors and sounds produce fifty fundamental sounds, which, in the post-Shiva era, were translated into the sounds of the vowels and consonants of the Sanskrit language. All other compounded sounds originate from these fifty sounds and thus their collective name is the *causal matrix*. From these fifty sounds, mantras were developed, which allowed a person to resonate and activate the different chakras and thereby elevate his or her consciousness. This process is called raising the Kundalini. The sound vibrations of the mantras act to vibrate the glands of the body and awaken the energy from dormancy. Upon being awakened, the energy rises up through the spine, creating tremendous force, as well as spiritual powers that include the control of matter, liquid, fire, air, and ether. The highest chakra, the *sahasra'ra chakra*, which is referred to as the thousand-petal lotus, controls one thousand propensities. It controls all the lower chakras. When this chakra is activated, the pineal gland, which is located in the crown of the brain, releases a hormone that induces an indescribable spiritual ecstasy in the human being. The yogis call this blissful intoxication Samadhi; the Buddhists call it Nirvana. When one is able to achieve this state at will, that person is becomes enlightened or God-realized. For that person, there is no longer a within or without, no I or thou. All is One.

Shiva was often in the state of divine ecstasy, and people sometime took him for being intoxicated on drugs or alcohol. This is why he is often associated with wine and revelry. Dionysius and Bacchus, who were Greek gods derived from Shiva, reflect this spiritual intoxication.[148]

Long before Shiva, when people began to offer sacrifices, they recognized the existence of the Goddess or the God, but they did not know how to attain this Divinity. They did not know how to develop God-consciousness, nor make themselves fit instruments for the attainment of the Supreme. Shiva prepared the path of spiritual practice for people and taught them how to evolve their minds with the help of love, marriage, service, dance, music, medicine, and, most importantly, the concept of dharma and the practice of mantra. The fundamental meaning of mantras is *I am one with the One*. It is this ideation, performed with love in the heart that moves people toward Divinity. It is the *dharma* or nature of human beings to become Divine.[149]

It is fair to say that before Shiva a spiritual science did not exist. With the coming of Shiva, everyone finally had access to a clear path toward spiritual realization. Shiva's teachings have come down to us through many religions and they continue to provide these religions with their spiritual inspiration. This occurred despite the fact that there was no written language at the time that Shiva lived in India.

Because of such accomplishments and because of his great love for humanity and all forms of life, the majority of the people came to accept Shiva as Mahadeva, the Lord of the lords.

What is the relationship between Sadashiva and Cosmic Consciousness? Shrii P. R. Sarkar made this observation:

The present, which is the result of the convergence of past and future, will certainly be recognized by the undulation of waves in the infinite cosmic body. And the Supreme Consciousness, in whose vast bosom these undulations of the so-called present rise and fall, is seeing all the stages of this vibrational flow, is knowing them, and, by His sacred witness-ship, making their existences flow with sweetness. Thus, Sadashiva, the repository of cognition, knows everything that has been thus far created. And that which is yet to be, is the impending result of the cosmic laws of causation.[150]

We can see now that the ritual sacrifices of the Arsa Dharma (Religion of the Sages), created by the Aryans, did not hold a candle to the bright sun of Shaeva Dharma. Over time, the Vedas were compelled to change in order to accommodate the teachings of Shiva. Even so, a fundamental difference between the Vedas and Tantra has existed since the beginning. The Vedas granted primary importance to race and class differences, while Tantra granted importance only to the ideal human being. There was very little scope for spiritual development in the animal sacrifices and prayerful Aryan religion, which is why the Aryans who settled in India gradually came to adapt the spiritual practices of Tantra. The effectiveness of Tantra in developing one's personality and vigor, within a short span of time, made it attractive to the Aryans. In the beginning, therefore, many Aryan's began practicing Tantra in secrecy.

For the descendents of the Aryans who continue to place emphasis on sexism, racism, and castism in the name of religion, their motivation is only to exploit the people and not to encourage them to be greater human beings. These exploiters will eventually be revealed for who they are, and people will rebel against them.

It is hoped that in this brief presentation the difference between religion and spirituality was made clear. In spirituality, it is not possible to divide humanity. Religion, on the other hand, is often the cause and aggravation of superficial differences in order to exploit people for wealth and power. Spirituality (mysticism) is synthetic; it seeks unity. Religion is analytic; it focuses on differences and exploits them. An analytic perspective brings divisions, and divisive tendencies create impediments to peace. The only way to save human beings and the natural world going forward is to adopt the path of synthesis. There is no other way than this.

Any religion can surely benefit by incorporating yogic spiritual practices. But spiritual practitioners have nothing essential to gain from religion other than it may provide them with a *style* of worship that soothes their heart. For example, a Christian mystic, Buddhist mystic, Jain mystic, or Jewish mystic may all find comfort in using the form of their religion as a mode to increase their spirituality. But if they are true mystics, they will recognize their kinship with all humanity, regardless of their religion. This kinship is based on the fact that they are all working to shorten the distance between their individual consciousness and the Macrocosmic Consciousness through meditation (contemplation) and selfless service.

The spiritual science of Tantric mysticism, which suffused Eastern culture, made its way slowly to the West throughout the following millennia, carried by traders, mystics, and Aryan war parties. Ideas of Eastern spirituality impacted Zoroaster and through him the Jews. It also impacted the Greeks whose mystery religions would merge with early Christianity to give impetus to the early Gnostics and, through them, the Orthodox Christian Church and, to some extent, even the Catholic Church of Rome.

# Notes

1. "7 Medieval African Kingdoms Everyone Should Know About," *Atlantic Black Star*, December 5, 2013, http://atlantablackstar.com/2013/12/05/7-midieval-african-kingdoms/.
2. Wikipedia, "Recent African Origins of Modern Humans," accessed May 22, 2018 https://en.wikipedia.org/wiki/Recent_African_origin_of_modern_humans.
3. "Pre-Colonial America: BC – 1607 AD," accessed May 22, 2018, http://storiesofusa.com/pre-colonial-america/.
4. "Timeline of human evolution," Wikipedia, last modified February 14, 2018, http://en.wikipedia.org/wiki/Timeline_of_human_evolution.
5. New Scientist, "Dawn of Human Race Uncovered," last modified June 11, 2003, https://www.newscientist.com/article/dn3814-dawn-of-human-race-uncovered/.
6. Wikipedia, "Human," accessed February 11, 2018, https://en.wikipedia.org/wiki/Human.
7. Christian, David, *Big History: Between Nothing and Everything* (New York: McGraw Hill Education, 2004), 93. Referenced in http://en.wikipedia.org/wiki/Paleolithic.
8. Hillary Mayell, "When Did 'Modern' Behavior Emerge in Humans?" *National Geographic News*. Retrieved 2008-02-05. Referenced in http://en.wikipedia.org/wiki/Paleolithic.
9. Hillary Mayell, "When Did 'Modern' Behavior Emerge in Humans?"
10. John Weinstock, "Sami Prehistory Revisited: transactions, admixture and assimilation in the phylogeographic picture of Scandinavia." Referenced in http://en.wikipedia.org/wiki/Paleolithic.
11. John Weinstock, *Sami Prehistory Revisited*.
12. Julian Jaynes, *The Origins of Consciousness in the Breakdown of the Bicameral Mind* (Boston: Houghton Mifflin Co., 1976), 130-131.
13. P. R. Sarkar, "To the Patriots," in *Prout in a Nutshell Volume 1 Part 4, 1st Edition*. (Jamalpur: Ananda Marga Publication, 1960)

14. H. L. Mencken, *Treatise on the Gods*, (New York: Blue Ribbon Books, 1930), 84.
15. Robert Briffault, *The Mothers:The Matriarchal Theory of Social Origins, Vol. I* (New York: Howard Fertig Publishers, 1993), 191.
16. P. R. Sarkar, "How to Unite Human Society," in *Prout in a Nutshell Volume 4 Part 21 [a compilation]*, (Patna: Ananda Marga Publications, 1970).
17. Evelyn Reed, *Woman's Evolution: From Matriarchal Clan to Patriarchal Family* (Atlanta: Pathfinder Press, 1975).
18. Marimba Ani, *Yurugu: An African-Centered Critique of European Cultural Thought and Behavior*, (Africa World Press, 1994).
19. Jaynes, *The Origins of Consciousness*.
20. "African Goddesses," listed at http://www.lowchensaustralia.com/names/african-goddesses.htm.
21. Barbara G. Walker, *The Woman's Encyclopedia of Myths and Secrets*. San Francisco: Harper Row, 1983), 518.
22. Wikipedia, "Dikta" accessed April 17, 2017, http://en.wikipedia.org/wiki/Dikti.
23. Walker, *The Woman's Encyclopedia*, 381.
24. "The Gods and Goddesses of Africa," http://www.scns.com/earthen/other/seanachaidh/godafrica.html.
25. "Gods and Goddesses of Ancient India," http://www.crystalinks.com/indiadieties.html.
26. Walker, *The Woman's Encyclopedia*, 487.
27. Walker, *The Woman's Encyclopedia*, 1018.
28. Walker, *The Woman's Encyclopedia*, 38.
29. Walker, *The Woman's Encyclopedia*, 38.
30. Walker, *The Woman's Encyclopedia*, 768.
31. Walker, *The Woman's Encyclopedia*, 903.
32. Walker, *The Woman's Encyclopedia*, 903.
33. Wikipedia, "Naga", accessed February 14, 2018, http://en.wikipedia.org/wiki/N%C4%81ga.
34. Walker, *The Woman's Encyclopedia*, 903.
35. Walker, *The Woman's Encyclopedia*, 903.
36. Walker, *The Woman's Encyclopedia*, 903-4.
37. The *Rg Veda*, "HYMN XXXII. Indra," accessed February 19, 2018, http://www.sacred-texts.com/hin/rigveda/rv01032.htm.
38. Walker, *The Woman's Encyclopedia*, 877.
39. Wikipedia, "Romulus and Remus," accessed February 19, 2018,

http://en.wikipedia.org/wiki/Romulus_and_Remus.
40. Walker, *The Woman's Encyclopedia*, 501.
41. Walker, *The Woman's Encyclopedia*, 502.
42. Walker, *The Woman's Encyclopedia*, 502.
43. Walker, *The Woman's Encyclopedia*, 30.
44. Leonard Cottrell, *The Concise Encyclopedia Of Archaeology*, First Edition (New York: Hawthorne Books, 1960), http://www.apologeticspress.org/rr/reprints/ras-shamra.pdf.
45. Walker, *The Woman's Encyclopedia*, 71.
46. Walker, *The Woman's Encyclopedia*, 685.
47. Walker, *The Woman's Encyclopedia*, 897.
48. Walker, *The Woman's Encyclopedia*, 681.
49. Walker, *The Woman's Encyclopedia*, 682.
50. Walker, *The Woman's Encyclopedia*, 682.
51. Walker, *The Woman's Encyclopedia*, 684.
52. Walker, *The Woman's Encyclopedia*, 685.
53. Walker, *The Woman's Encyclopedia*, 688.
54. Lewis Mumford, *Interpretations and Forecasts,* (New York: Harcourt, Brace Jovanovich, 1973), 347-48.
55. George Gilder, *Naked Nomads: Unmarried Men in America*, (New York: Quadrangle/New York Times Book Co., 1974).
56. Walker, *The Woman's Encyclopedia*, 680.
57. Evelyn Reed, *Woman's Evolution: From Matriarchal Clan to Patriarchal Family*, (Atlanta: Pathfinder Press, 1975), 218.
58. Reed, *Woman's Evolution*, 223.
59. Reed, *Woman's Evolution*, 216.
60. "Peaceful Societies," *UAB College of Arts and Sciences*, accessed at February, 19, 2018, https://cas.uab.edu/peacefulsocieties/2016/03/03/10346/.
61. R. F. Fortune, *Sorcerers of Dobu*, (Oxon Australia, Routledge,1932), 23-24.
62. Reed, *Woman's Evolution*, 304.
63. Reed, *Woman's Evolution*, 305.
64. Reed, *Woman's Evolution*,306.
65. Reed, *Woman's Evolution*, 311.
66. Fortune, *Sorcerers of Dobu*, 22.
67. Reed, *Woman's Evolution*, 322.
68. Reed, *Woman's Evolution*, 394.
69. Reed, *Woman's Evolution*, 343-344.

70. Reed, *Woman's Evolution*, 395.
71. Reed, *Woman's Evolution*, 396.
72. Widipedia, "Fratricide," accessed January 14, 2018, http://en.wikipedia.org/wiki/Fratricide.
73. Ivan Strenski, ed., *Malinowski and the Work of Myth* (Princeton: Princeton University Press, 1936), 66.
74. Reed, *Woman's Evolution*, 397.
75. William Graham Sumner, *Folkways: A Study of Mores, Manners, Customs and Morals*,(New York: Cosimo Classics, 2007), Referenced in Reed, *Women's Evolution*, 398.
76. Lloyd deMause, *The Emotional Life of Nations* (NY/London: Karnak, 2002), last modified August 7, 2017, https://en.wikipedia.org/wiki/Early_infanticidal_childrearing.
77. "Firstborn," *Jewish Virtual Library*, accessed February 20, 2018, http://www.jewishvirtuallibrary.org/jsource/judaica/ejud_0002_0007_0_06494.html.
78. Reed, *Women's Evolution*, 402-403.
79. Reed, *Women's Evolution*, 406.
80. Reed, *Women's Evolution*, 406.
81. Robert Briffault, *The Mothers, Vol. II*, (New York: The Macmillan Co. 1927), 218.
82. Reed, *Women's Evolution*, 414.
83. Reed, *Women's Evolution*, 417.
84. Renu Agal, "India's 'bride buying' country," *BBC News*, April 2006, https://en.wikipedia.org/wiki/Bride_buying.
85. "End Forced Marriage in the United States," *Change.org*, accessed February 20, 2018, https://www.change.org/p/president-of-the-united-states-end-forced-marriage-in-the-united-states?utm_source=action_alert&utm_medium=email&utm_campaign=262431&alert_id=VX-HtMgAFuN_9tr9aEZaAjYGi65nld%2F8zPWhz6Slf7zQNortJR6oL-COoFYJ6FjXIXrR66zaz%2BtN%2B.
86. Reed, *Women's Evolution*, 420.
87. Reed, *Women's Evolution*, 423.
88. E. Adamson Hoebel, *Man In The Primitive World*, (New York: McGraw-Hill, 1958), 208.
89. Reed, *Women's Evolution*, 429.
90. Briffault, *The Mothers I*, 345.
91. Harking back to its ancient past, the Aryan Hindu tradition maintains fire as the center of every ritual. The initiation into Hinduism is

the right to light the fire, marriage is solemnized by striding around the fire and in death the corpse is cremated.
92. P. R. Sarkar, "Casteism and the Decline of Womens Status Section D," published in *The Awakening of Women (a compilation)* (Kolkata: Ananda Marga Publication, 1985).
93. "The Khasia," *Bangladesh News*, accessed February, 20, 2018, http://www.independent-bangladesh.com/ethnic-groups/the-khasia.html.
94. P. R. Sarkar, "The Vipra Age," *Human Society II* (Kolkata, Ananda Marga Publications, 1967).
95. P. R. Sarkar, "Tantra and Indo-Aryan Civilization," May 1959, RU, Muzaffarpur, *A Few Problems Solved Part 1*, (Kolkata: Ananda Marga publications, 2009).
96. P. R. Sarkar "Shiva – Both Severe and Tender (Discourse 2)," *Namah Shivaya Shantaya* (Kolkata: Ananda Marga Publications, 1982).
97. Sarkar, *Shiva*.
98. Sarkar, *Shiva*.
99. *Rg Veda*, "[10-090] HYMN XC. Purusa," accessed February 20, 2018, http://www.sanskritweb.net/rigveda/griffith.pdf.
100. Lindsay Jones, et. al., *Encyclopedia of religion*. (Detroit: Macmillan Reference, 2005), 201.
101. Jones, *Encyclopedia of religion*, 201.
102. Jones, *Encyclopedia of religion*, 203.
103. *Rg Veda*, Hymn xxxii Indra, last accessed February 20, 2018, http://www.sacred-texts.com/hin/rigveda/rv01032.htm.
104. Wikipedia, "Proto-Indo-European Religion," accessed February 20, 2018, http://en.wikipedia.org/wiki/Proto-Indo-European_religion.
105. *Rg Veda*, "Hymn cxxxiii," accessed February 20, 2018, http://www.sacred-texts.com/hin/rigveda/rv01133.htm.
106. *Rg Veda*, "Hymn x Indra," accessed February 20, 2018, http://www.sacred-texts.com/hin/rigveda/rv01010.htm.
107. *Rg Veda*, "Hymn cii," accessed February 20, 2018, http://www.sacred-texts.com/hin/rigveda/rv01102.htm.
108. *Rg Veda*, 'Hymn cii,' accessed February 20, 2018, http://www.sacred-texts.com/hin/rigveda/rv01029.htm.
109. Jones, *The Encyclopedia of Religions*, 210.
110. Wikipedia, "Mehrgarh," accessed January 24, 2018, http://en.wikipedia.org/wiki/Mehrgarh.
111. Wikipedia, "Mehrgarh."
112. Wikipedia, "Mehrgarh."

113. M. C. Joshi, "Historical and Iconographical Aspects of Shakta Tantrism." Referenced in Katherine Harper, (ed.), *The Roots of Tantra*, (Albany, State University of New York Press, 2002), 39.
114. Jane McIntosh, *"The Ancient Indus Valley: New Perspectives,"* ABC-CLIO, 2008, 387.
115. Upinder Singh, *A History of Ancient and Early medieval India: from the Stone Age to the 12th century* (New Delhi: Pearson Education, 2008), 137.
116. Wikipedia, "Indus Valley Civilization," accessed February 18, 2018, http://en.wikipedia.org/wiki/Indus_Valley_Civilization.
117. Joseph Campbell, *Oriental Mythology: The Masks of God*, (New York: Penguin Press, 1969), 166-167.
118. G Robbins Schug, K Elaine Blevins, Brett Cox, Kelsey Gray, and V Mushrif-Tripathy (2013) "Infection, Disease, and Biosocial Process at the End of the Indus Civilization," *Journals.Plos.One*, last accessed February 20, 2018, http://journals.plos.org/plosone/article?id=10.1371/journal.pone.0084814.
119. Wikipedia, "Mohenjo-daro," accessed February 3, 2018, http://en.wikipedia.org/wiki/Mohenjo-daro.
120. Wikipedia, "Dancing Girl (sculpture)," accessed April 14, 2018, https://en.wikipedia.org/wiki/Dancing_Girl_(sculpture).
121. Wikipedia, "Mohenjo-daro."
122. Joseph Campbell, *Oriental Mythology: The Masks of God*, 158-159.
123. Wikipedia, "Mohenjo-daro."
124. Campbell, *Oriental Mythology*, 172-173.
125. Campbell, *Oriental Mythology*, 174.
126. Campbell, *Oriental Mythology*, 174.
127. P. R .Sarkar, "Kuta_to_Kuttima_discourse_28,". *Shabda Cayaniká Part 5*, (Kolkata: Ananda Marga Publications, 1986).
128. P. R. Sarkar, *Rárh: The Cradle of Civilization* (Kolkata: Ananda Marga Publications, 1981).
129. Wikipedia, "Mitochondrial Eve," accessed February 19, 2018, http://en.wikipedia.org/wiki/Mitochondrial_Eve.
130. P. R. Sarkar, "Social Discourses 1957-1981", *The Thoughts of P. R. Sarkar [A Compilation]*, (Kolkata, Ananda Marga Publications. Date unknown.)
131. G. S. Gurye, *Caste and Race in India* (Mumbai: Popular Prakashan, 1969) 1-27, https://archive.org/details/in.ernet.dli.2015.69673.
132. P. R. Sarkar, "Religious Dogma Section B," *Prout in a Nutshell*

*Volume 4 Part 16*, (Kolkata: Ananda Marga Publications, 1988).
133. Wikipeida,"Caste system in India," accessed February 8, 2018, http://en.wikipedia.org/wiki/. Caste_system_in_India#CITEREFGhurye1969.
134. Wikipedia, "Sanskrit," accessed February 21, 2018, http://en.wikipedia.org/wiki/Sanskrit#Origin_and_development.
135. Sarkar, *Religious Dogma Section B*.
136. P. R. Sarkar, *Namah Shivaya Shantaya*, (Kolkata: Ananda Marga Publications, 1982), 104, See http://www.anandamargabooks.org/Namah%20Shivaya%20Shantaya.html.
137. Sarkar, *Namah Shivaya Shantaya*, 77.
138. Rabindranath Tagore, "The Beginning", translated in *Namah Shivaya Shantaya*, p 81-82.
139. See Volume II for an in-depth analysis of Jesus Christ as a God-realized human being.
140. Sarkar, *Namah Shivaya Shantaya*.
141. P R Sarkar, *Discourses on Tantra: Volume One*, (Kolkata: Ananda Marga Publications, 1993).
142. Sarkar, *Discourses on Tantra*, 308.
143. Sarkar, *Discourses on Tantra*, 14.
144. P. R. Sarkar. "Shiva in the Dhyána Mantra (Discourse 20)," *Namah Shivaya Sh.ántáya*. (Patna: Ananda Marga Publications, 1982).
145. "The Pervasive Influence of Shiva Continued," *Speakingtree.in*, accessed April 21, 2018, https://www.speakingtree.in/blog/the-pervasive-influence-of-shiva-continued.
146. Wikipedia, "Pashupati," accessed February 15, 2018, https://en.wikipedia.org/wiki/Pashupati.
147. P. R. Sarkar. "Parvatii Consort of Shiva Section A," *The Awakening of Women [a compilation]*. (Kolkata: Ananda Marga Publications, 1982).
148. Alain Daniélou, *Gods of Love and Ecstasy: The Traditions of Shiva and Dionysus*, (Rochester VT: Inner Traditions, 1992).
149. Sarkar, *Namah Shivaya Shantaya*.
150. Sarkar, *Namah Shivaya Shantaya*, 235.

# Index

## A

Aberewa 32
Abraham 66
Acadians 36, 102
Adam 78
aegis 41
Afghanistan 75, 91, 92, 98, 101
Africa 9, 19, 21, 22, 23, 27, 30, 32, 53, 70, 72, 75, 76, 101, 123
Agean 36
Agni 83
agricultural civilizations 7, 17, 19, 27, 28, 50, 53, 87, 92, 95
agricultural economy 59
agriculture 10, 27, 42, 47, 48, 51, 53, 57, 71, 92, 95, 113
Aitareya Brahmana 84
Ajanta 31
Ala 32
Ale 32
Allahabad 99
alphabets 48
Alpine 101
Americas 10, 70
Ananta the Infinite 35
Anath 34, 41, 43
anathema 43
Andaman Islands 101
Ane 32
Angkor Wat 35
animal sacrifice 55, 66
Apollo 89
Arabs 102
Arctic Ocean 101
Arjuna 65
Armageddon 86

Arsa Dharma 82, 120
artifacts 8, 17, 22, 92, 94, 95
Aryans 24, 32, 33, 43, 62, 77, 78, 80, 81, 82, 83, 85, 86, 87, 89, 90, 91, 92, 94, 95, 97, 98, 99, 100, 101, 102, 103, 107, 108, 109, 110, 116, 117, 118, 120, 121
Asase 32
ascetics 46
Ashurbanipal 39
Asia 72, 75, 76, 81, 92, 93, 101, 102, 116
Assyria 39
astral bodies 42
astronomy/astrology 42
asuras 117
Atharvaveda 107
Athena 41
Australia 72, 101, 124
Australoid 100, 102
Austric Munda 95
Austrics 101
Ayurveda 116
Aztecs 68

## B

Baal 89
Babylon 39
Babylonians 36
Bacchus 119
Baluchistan 92
Bellerophon 89
Benares 99
Bengal 114
Benin 9, 30
Beowulf 89
Bering Strait 10, 101

birth 5, 6, 9, 11, 19, 29, 30, 31, 33, 34, 35, 37, 42, 43, 47, 51, 62, 104
Black Sea 91
Blombos Cave 23
blood 7, 29, 35, 36, 37, 38, 39, 40, 41, 42, 43, 44, 46, 51, 52, 53, 54, 63, 64, 65, 66, 67, 68, 71, 81, 102, 108, 117
blood gift 66
blood redemption 65, 66, 67, 68
blood revenge 53, 54, 63, 66, 71
Bomo Rambi 30
Borneo 101
Brahmanas 107
Brahmins 103
bride price 72, 73, 74, 75, 76, 78
Briffault's Law 25
British Isles 101
brother 25, 26, 52, 56, 57, 58, 59, 60, 61, 62, 63, 64, 65, 66, 67, 70, 71, 72, 73, 75, 76, 77, 80, 83, 86
Buddhists 110, 119
Burma 101
Buruku 30

## C

Cabiria 46
Cambodians 35
Canaan 40
Canaanites 34, 68, 102
Carnival 45
Carthaginians 66, 68
Caspian Sea 91
caste system 94, 99, 103, 104, 105, 106
castrated 43, 67
cattle 72, 73, 74, 76, 77, 81, 84, 90, 91, 92, 94
cattle marriage 73, 74
cattle raids 91
Caucasian 24, 81, 82, 100
Caucasoid 100, 101, 102

Caucasus Mountains 21, 81
cave art 30
caves 23, 30, 31, 32, 34, 35, 52
celibates 46
Center for Archaeological Research 92
Central Asia 75, 81, 116
Ceto 89
chakras 35, 118, 119
Chamber of Instruction 47
chariot 24, 98
child marriages 75
child price 74
children 7, 15, 21, 25, 38, 39, 48, 50, 56, 57, 58, 60, 61, 62, 63, 64, 66, 67, 72, 73, 74, 75, 76, 77, 78, 79, 80, 95, 98, 100, 114, 115
child sacrifice 66
Chimera 89
China 9, 75, 101
Chineke 32
Christ 8, 11, 19, 34, 89, 128
Christian 19, 31, 34, 45, 49, 89, 121, 122
Christianity 11, 46, 86, 121
civilization 1, 6, 12, 17, 19, 24, 27, 33, 42, 46, 48, 91, 92, 95, 101, 106, 108, 113, 117
clan 7, 15, 18, 24, 26, 27, 30, 32, 39, 51, 54, 56, 57, 60, 61, 65, 66, 71, 73, 79, 81
class-based society 69
classification of married women 78
classism 106, 114
class system 84, 103
Code of Hammurabi 74
cognitive principle 109
Colombia 102
combat 54, 55
confederation 7, 27, 51, 57
Congo 30
counter punishment 53

couvade 62, 63
creation myth 43, 83
Crete 31, 40
crone 37, 46
cross cousin 61
Cybele 31
cycle 28, 29, 33, 37, 42, 43
cyclical warfare 54

## D

Daksha 117
dance of death 55
Danu 87, 88
Danube Valley 101
dasa 100
Dasas 87
day 5, 20, 24, 26, 32, 37, 42, 46, 48, 66, 81, 86, 98, 99, 115
death 28, 31, 32, 33, 40, 41, 42, 43, 44, 45, 46, 53, 54, 55, 57, 61, 62, 63, 77, 85, 86, 87, 89, 90, 105, 110, 126
demos 52
dentistry 94
dharma 119
Dionysius 119
divinity 27, 32, 38, 68, 86, 108
DNA 3, 100
dowry 74, 78
dragon 86, 87, 89
Dravidian 31, 80, 87, 91, 95, 104, 107, 108, 109, 113
Durga 30
Dyaus Pitar 83

## E

Earth Goddess 31
Efua 32
Egypt 7, 9, 17, 28, 36, 50, 53, 59, 66, 83, 92, 101
Egyptian 47, 89, 101
El 89

Elephanta 31
Eleusis 46
Ellora 31
Encyclopedia of Religions 84, 126
Erua 39
Essenes 108
Etruscans 45
Europe 5, 9, 17, 19, 23, 24, 34, 52, 70, 72, 76, 83, 91, 100, 101, 107
Eve 78, 101, 127
expiatory combat 54

## F

Fafnir 89
Far East 9, 53, 70
farming 32, 59, 72
Fat-Frumos 89
father 7, 19, 25, 26, 31, 36, 38, 39, 43, 44, 50, 56, 59, 61, 62, 63, 64, 65, 66, 67, 68, 69, 70, 73, 74, 75, 76, 77, 78, 79, 80, 83, 114, 115, 117
father-family 19, 56, 59, 63, 64, 68, 69, 76, 77, 78
fatherhood 36, 62, 74
father-rule 26, 70, 80
feasts 44
female 21, 23, 24, 25, 26, 27, 28, 35, 48, 51, 70, 77, 93, 94, 95
female-fathers 77
female-husband 77
fertility 11, 18, 28, 40, 44, 46, 110
figurines 23, 92, 93
firstborn son 65, 66, 67
Folkways 65, 125
forced marriages 75
France 101
Fratriarchy 52
fratricide 64

## G

Gabriel 89

Gaia  30, 31
Ganesha  108
Ganges  99
Garden of Eden  34, 47, 50, 78, 86
Gaunga  114
gender  1, 7, 16, 18, 24, 26, 50, 56, 70, 92, 95
Ghana  9, 30
ghee  82
ghost  65, 67, 76
ghost marriage  76
gift exchange  54, 55, 58, 71, 72, 73
Gleti  30
god  12, 18, 19, 29, 39, 44, 45, 78, 82, 83, 85, 86, 89, 108, 109, 110, 111
goddess  28, 29, 30, 31, 33, 34, 35, 45, 67, 93
Goddess Rhea  31
goddess worship  30
gotra  79, 80, 81, 104, 113, 114
Great Goddess  7, 18, 19, 27, 28, 31, 32, 33, 34, 39, 40, 41, 48, 51, 67, 86, 87, 93, 94, 108
Greece  52, 55
Guardian Ghost  67

## H

Harappa  93, 94, 95, 97
harvest  33, 38, 40
Hel  31
Hellenic  101, 108
Heracles  89
hereditary feud  54
hieros gamos  45
Hinduism  11, 35, 93, 105, 107, 108, 125
Hittite  89
human consciousness  10, 28, 42
human sacrifice  39, 66
husband  39, 56, 57, 58, 59, 60, 61, 62, 63, 64, 67, 71, 72, 73, 74, 75, 76, 77, 78, 79, 114, 117

husbandry  32, 59
Hydra  89

## I

Iishvara  110
Illuyanka  89
immortality  34, 35, 47, 68
Incas  68
India  9, 17, 24, 31, 32, 35, 42, 43, 53, 75, 77, 78, 80, 81, 83, 87, 91, 92, 93, 94, 97, 98, 99, 100, 101, 102, 103, 104, 105, 106, 108, 110, 111, 114, 116, 117, 118, 120, 123, 125, 127, 128
Indian Ocean  101
Indian Subcontinent  92
Indochina  101
Indra  36, 84, 85, 86, 87, 88, 89, 90, 91, 109, 123, 126
Indus River  92, 93, 94, 97
Indus Valley  7, 17, 19, 21, 24, 28, 33, 50, 83, 89, 91, 92, 93, 94, 95, 98, 101, 107, 117, 127
interbreeding  100
Iran  92, 101
iron bangles  81
Ishme-Dagan  39
Ishtar  39
Islam  11, 86
Isle of Crete  31
Israelites  66

## J

Jains  110
Japan  9, 23, 101
Java  101
Jesus  8, 11, 14, 19, 34, 112, 128
Joseph Campbell  97, 98, 127
Judaism  11, 86

## K

Kabul  98

Kacchi Plain 92
Kadi of Der 36
Kadru 35
Kala-Nath 33, 42
Kali 31, 33, 108
Kalii 114
Karna 65
Kashmir 91, 98, 101
killing the firstborn son 65
kin 53, 58, 60, 63, 64
king 5, 7, 39, 40, 41, 42, 43, 44, 45, 46, 56, 64, 68, 83, 84, 85, 86, 95, 99
King Esarkaddon 39
King of Isin 39
kings 39, 40, 41, 44, 46, 56, 68
kingship 39
kinship 50, 53, 56, 63, 64, 67, 121
kinsman 54
Kolkata 99, 126, 127, 128
Kronos 89
Ksattriyans 103
Kundalini 35, 119
Kurukulla 31

## L

Ladon 89
Lady of the Serpent Skirt 41
Lat 52
latifundia 52
Leviathan 89
leviratic marriage 76, 77
life cycle 33, 37, 42
lifespan 42
Lord of Death 43, 44
Lotan 89
lunar calendar 42

## M

Magadha 99
magic 7, 30, 32, 42, 44, 53, 61, 67
magical knowledge 37, 46, 63

magical signs 48
Mahabharata 117
Malayalese 80
Malayan Peninsula 101
male 5, 17, 21, 24, 25, 36, 38, 41, 44, 46, 50, 51, 55, 56, 57, 58, 60, 63, 66, 67, 68, 69, 70, 71, 73, 77, 78, 79, 84, 86, 89, 97, 114, 115
male deities 36
male-mother 56, 57
male priestesses 56
male-priestesses 67
male rule 56, 70
mandalas 48
Man In The Primitive World 77, 125
Marduk 89
Marimba Ani 27, 123
marriage 45, 46, 57, 58, 59, 61, 62, 70, 71, 72, 73, 74, 75, 76, 77, 78, 79, 80, 81, 82, 104, 105, 114, 117, 119, 125, 126
marriage gift 72
martyrs 44
Mat Chinoi 35
maternal uncle 65, 73
mathematici 42
mathematics 7, 10, 27, 42, 43, 48, 94, 113
Mathura 99
matra 42
Matriarchy iii, 21, 22
matrilineal system 80
matrimony 58
Medes 83
Mediterranean 23, 101
Mehrgarh 92, 93, 126
menstrual blood 29, 36, 38, 41
Mesopotamia 7, 17, 28, 50, 53, 74, 83, 92, 98
Mestizo 102
meter 43, 115
Mexico 102

Michael the Archangel 89
Michelangelo 86
Middle East 9, 17, 19, 24, 53, 66, 68, 70, 75, 76, 83, 91, 107, 108
Mistress of Serpents 36
Mithila 99
Mithraism 86
Mitochondrial Eve 101, 127
Mohenjo-daro 93, 95, 96, 97, 98, 127
Molochs 67
Mongolians 101
Mongoloid 100, 102
month 29, 38, 42, 48
moon 29, 30, 31, 32, 36, 40, 84
Moon Goddess 30
Mot/Aleyin 43
mother 25, 26, 28, 31, 34, 35, 37, 42, 43, 46, 47, 48, 50, 54, 56, 57, 58, 59, 60, 61, 62, 63, 64, 65, 66, 67, 68, 71, 73, 74, 76, 77, 79, 80, 88, 93, 95, 101, 103, 114
Mother Earth 30
mother-family 56, 59, 60, 63, 68
Motherhood 28
mother-in-law 58, 59
mother-rule 26, 28, 50, 80
Mount Dicte 31
mudra 115
mysticism 10, 13, 19, 82, 91, 121
myths 13, 22, 26, 33, 34, 35, 37, 40, 41, 43, 64, 65, 86, 100, 108

# N

Nagas 35
Namah Shivaya Shantaya 112, 126, 128
Nataraj 116
Natha 110
nationality 1, 2, 11, 18, 70
nations 7, 10, 15, 27, 32, 39, 65, 78
Native Americans 101, 102

Negritos 35
Negroes 101
Negroid 100, 101, 102, 114, 117
Neolithic culture 92
nephews 64, 65
New Delhi 98, 127
New Guinea 75, 101
New York City 103
night 29, 32, 37, 47, 48, 57, 58, 59
Ninhursag 36
Nirguna Brahma 109
Nordic 17, 24, 101
North America 101
Nzambi 30

# O

ochre 23, 38, 93
octave 115
Old Testament 36, 74
operative principle 109
Ophion 89
Ophite Christianity 46
oracles 68
orgiastic rituals 37
orgies 45, 46
own 4, 6, 25, 28, 30, 37, 38, 39, 57, 58, 60, 61, 64, 68, 71, 73, 76, 77, 78, 85, 87, 95, 105, 114, 115, 116, 117
owner 62, 72, 74, 78
ownership 55, 56, 62, 65, 70, 74, 77, 114

# P

Pair-union 58
Pakistan 91, 92, 93, 98, 101
Paleolithic Age 22, 23, 51, 52
Palestine 101
Paoranik Age 110
Papua New Guinea 75
paradise 34, 36, 47, 92
Parama Purusha 112

Paris  92
Parvatii  114, 128
Pashupati  97, 115, 118, 128
Passover  66
Patnii  79
patriarchal religions  21, 46, 47, 71
patriarchal society  7, 22, 55, 76, 77
Patriarchy  70, 71
penises  41
Perseus  89
Persians  16, 31, 83
Per-Uatchet  36
Perun  89
phallic worship  110
phallus  37
Philippines  75, 101
Phyrigians  31
pictographs  48
pitched battle  54
Pleistocene  23, 52
Prakriti  109
Pratiloma  79
prearranged combat  54
priestesses  28, 41, 42, 43, 56, 67
Priest-King  97
principle of equivalence  54
property  7, 17, 19, 49, 52, 55, 56, 61, 62, 64, 67, 68, 69, 70, 72, 73, 74, 75, 76, 77, 78, 87, 100
Puranas  107
pure race  100, 102
Purusa  84, 126
Purusha  83, 85, 109, 112
Python  89

Q

queen  39, 40, 44, 68
Quetzalcoatl  41

R

Rabindranath Tagore  111, 128

race  1, 3, 4, 11, 16, 18, 24, 53, 70, 81, 92, 100, 101, 102, 115, 120, 122
racism  100, 102, 103, 106, 114, 121
Rahab  89
Ranchi  99
Rarh  99
Ras Shamra texts  41
Ra vs. Apep  89
redemptive sacrifice  65
regulated fight  54
regulated punishment  53
reincarnation  33, 42
religion  1, 5, 8, 12, 16, 18, 20, 28, 69, 70, 82, 85, 92, 93, 102, 107, 108, 110, 120, 121, 126
religious dogma  5, 105
resurrection  44, 86
Rg Veda  83, 85, 86, 87, 98, 107, 108, 115, 123, 126
Rhea  31
rituals  13, 23, 26, 28, 30, 31, 32, 33, 37, 42, 44, 45, 46, 48, 51, 69, 82, 91, 103, 110, 113
Rome  19, 31, 39, 64, 83, 86, 121
Romulus and Remus  39, 64, 123

S

sacer  38
sacred  7, 37, 38, 39, 40, 41, 42, 43, 44, 45, 46, 56, 64, 68, 84, 85, 86, 87, 91, 95, 120, 123, 126
sacred king  7, 39, 40, 42, 43, 44, 45, 46, 56, 68, 84, 95
sacrifice  7, 38, 39, 40, 41, 44, 45, 46, 55, 65, 66, 67, 83, 84, 85, 86, 89, 95
Sadashiva  110, 112, 120
Saguna Brahma  109
Saint George  89
Samaveda  107
Sanskrit  40, 42, 107, 118, 128
Saptasindhu  98
Sarasvati River  93

Satan  89
Saturn  45
Saturnalia  45
Savior  34, 42, 44
scapegoat  55
scepter  43, 44
second  14, 77, 86, 88, 98, 103, 112
Semites  101
Semitic  41, 62, 101
serpent  34, 35, 36, 47, 86, 89
sexism  106, 121
sexual countenance  46
sexual intercourse  58
sexual relations  57, 58, 100, 102
Shaeva Dharma  120
Shaivism  108
Shakti  108, 109
Shaktism  46, 93, 108
Shamash-shum-ukin  39
Shatadru  98
Shiva  9, 11, 19, 91, 97, 99, 107, 108, 109, 110, 111, 112, 113, 114, 115, 116, 117, 118, 119, 120, 126, 128
Shivagotra  113
Shivi  98
shruti  82
Shudras  103
Sibyl  31
Sigurd  89
Sind  98
sister  56, 60, 61, 63, 64, 65, 66, 67, 71, 72, 76
Sistine Chapel  86
skeletons  98
slavery  11, 16, 20, 81, 100
slaves  14, 76, 77, 78, 81, 84, 85, 87, 98, 99, 100, 102, 103, 117
Smartism  108
smriti  108
snake  35, 36
social psychology  11, 105, 106
socio-sentiment  100, 102

Solomon Islands  75
soma  90, 91
son  43, 44, 59, 63, 64, 65, 66, 67, 71, 74, 76, 77, 86, 88
Song of Purusha  83, 85
son-in-law  59, 71
Sorcerers of Dobu  57, 124
South America  102
Spain  101
species  3, 7, 11, 12, 17, 18, 21, 22, 23, 24, 41, 42, 47, 50, 70
sperm  29, 40, 51
spirit  29, 30, 32, 36, 45, 91
standup fight  54
star  40
state  5, 6, 11, 19, 21, 54, 56, 69, 71, 91, 98, 112, 119
Stone Age  22, 46, 127
Sufism  46
Sumatra  101
Sumeria  97
Sumerian  34, 101
Sun  12, 44, 87
Sun of Night  44
Surya  83, 108
Syria  41, 101

## T

Tandava  116
Tannin  89
Tantric  35, 91, 109, 112, 118, 121
Tara  33
Tarhunt  89
temenos  52
Thailand  75, 101
Thebes  40
Thor  89
Tiamat  89
Time  22, 48
totem  30, 36, 44
totemism  67
tree of immortality  47

tree of life  47
tribe  25, 27, 38, 40, 51, 57, 61, 62, 84, 85
two-father family  66
Typhon  89

## U

uncle  25, 61, 65, 71, 72, 73
underworld  31, 33, 43, 44, 45, 48
United States  iv, 2, 5, 20, 75, 100, 108, 125
units of measurement  48
untouchables  103, 111, 116
Upanishads  107
Uttar Pradesh  99

## V

vaedyak shastra  116
Vaeshyas  103
vaginas  38
Vaishnavism  108
Varanasi  99
Varuna  83
Vayu Purana  43
Vedas  36, 83, 86, 99, 107, 108, 112, 113, 120
Veles  89
vengeance fight  54
Venus of Willendorf  23
Videha  99
village  47, 57, 60, 61, 62, 79, 103
Vir  40
virgin  37, 46, 74, 75
Virgin  28, 33, 34
Vishnu  35, 108
Vitra  36, 86, 87, 88

## W

war  19, 49, 53, 55, 68, 85, 86, 91, 98, 109, 121
wealth  4, 13, 14, 16, 20, 32, 48, 51, 52, 53, 56, 61, 70, 71, 72, 90, 95, 103, 121
week  42, 48
weights and measures  94
West Africa  30
wheel of fortune  42
wheel of karma  42
wheel of rebirth  42
white supremacy  100
wife  58, 60, 61, 62, 63, 64, 67, 71, 72, 73, 74, 75, 76, 77, 78, 79, 114, 117
winter  28, 33, 37, 42, 44, 45
wolf  38, 39
woman-to-woman marriage  76, 77
Womb of Creation  33

## Y

Yaa  32
Yahweh  89
Yajurveda  107
Yam-Nahar  89
Yamuna  99
year  28, 40, 42, 43, 46, 48
yoga  91, 99, 108, 109, 110, 118
yogi  97

## Z

Zeus  31, 83, 89
Zimbabwe  30, 40
Zmeu  89
Zmey  89

# About The Authors

Charles Paprocki has spent many years working with troubled teenagers, prison inmates, welfare recipients, and migrant workers in the human services system. He also owned a graphics and advertising agency in New York City where he combined his skill and knowledge to create social marketing campaigns. He was one of the core leaders to create the Universal PreK program in New York State and the local food movement in Illinois. His last work was to manage an organic farm in southern Illinois. He has consulted with international NGOs on management strategies and participated in the Earth Summit in Brazil and the Social Summit in Denmark. He is now retired and living in Herrin, Illinois.

Tom Paprocki has worked several years in social services, including starting a preschool and daycare center in rural southern Illinois and serving as an administrator for a drug education and crisis center. After receiving a Masters in Public Administration, he was hired by the NASA Goddard Space Center as a Presidential Management Intern. He served thirty years at Goddard as head of Personnel, Procurement, and Institutional Resources. He spent the last seven years as Director of Management Operations, which included facilities, acquisitions, environmental and health services, security, and logistics for research and launch facilities at Greenbelt, Maryland and Wallops Island, Virginia.

www.ingramcontent.com/pod-product-compliance
Lightning Source LLC
Chambersburg PA
CBHW021111080526
44587CB00010B/476